POEMS'

❖

PROGRESS

POEMS'
❖
PROGRESS

WENDY BARKER

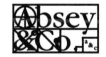

"That is question now;
And then comes answer like an Absey book.
King John, 1, 9
Shakespeare

OTHER BOOKS BY WENDY BARKER

POETRY
Way of Whiteness
Eve Remembers (a chapbook)
Let the Ice Speak
Winter Chickens

TRANSLATIONS
Rabindranath Tagore: Final Poems
        (with Saranindranath Tagore)

CRITICISM
The House Is Made of Poetry: The Art of Ruth Stone
        (with Sandra M. Gilbert)
Lunacy of Light: Emily Dickinson and the Experience of Metaphor

For David

ISBN 1-888842-35-0

Designed by Edward E. Wilson

About the Cover:
The art for the cover is titled *Still Life with Two Lemons* by Pieter Claesz, 1629. Sister Wendy Beckett says of the
painting: "What did Claesz actually see? This is not a breakfast, nor is it a lunch. What are the lemons doing there?
There is no fish or shellfish; and even if they are to be squeezed into the water or wine, three lemons is too many.
The olives also, at the back; what is their function? I began to realize that Claesz set this tableau up simply because he
likes the look of it. He wanted to paint those ovals; those subdued and gleaming hues; the fascinating ellipses of
plates, and circles on the glass. He rejoiced in the wet green of the olives and the yellow of the lemons—not just the
cut fruit, with its juicy rococo peel, but the massive, stage-stealing lemons in the center. They are the sole force of
vivacity. It is a long table, but he kept this little group anchored with the diagonal of a knife pointing in one direc-
tion, while the dark gleam of its sheath points in the other. The artist's enjoyment of what he arranged, his almost
rapturous response to the play of light over the varied textures: all this is infectious. It changes our way of looking.
Through Claesz, we see the work afresh." *Sister Wendy's American Collection*. New York: Harper Collins, 2000.

❖ PREFACE ❖

I did not at first want to write this book. Ed Wilson, editor and publisher of Absey & Co., asked me to. He was so encouraging, supportive, and flexible, I could not say no. Besides, my companion, Steven G. Kellman, an accomplished and prolific writer himself, had been urging me to tackle a prose project, insisting that working in prose as well as poetry would enhance my command of both genres. For a long time, I rejected my kindly scold's advice, whining, "Oh, you don't understand what a poet needs, I never have enough time even to write poems, just leave me alone."

I am grateful to Ed and to Steve. Because writing these essays turned out to be a joy. I still cannot imagine why anyone would want to read them; I have not yet written the kinds of poems I hope to, the kinds of poems that would cause readers to burn to know how a particular poem came to be. Someone once asked after a reading I had given, "What do you consider your best poem?" I answered without a breath of hesitation: "I haven't written it."

And I have not. A number of my poems I am pleased with, but most are simply poems that mark stages on the way to what I hope will be more worthy art. Some days I believe I will create something of lasting value before I die, and some days I do not. I am not sure what it is I am striving for, but I do know that if a poem changes me, or stays with me, it is an exceptional one. Many of Emily Dickinson's poems fall into that category, as do Whitman's, Yeats's, Stevens', Plath's, and Roethke's. (This is a highly abbreviated list; it could easily expand to fill this page.) Dickinson said poetry caused her to "feel physically as if the top of my head were taken off." I want to connect that viscerally through this musical, visual, and tactile art we call poetry, this art that can bypass the intellectual defenses often surrounding us like plexiglass shields. Good poetry hits us in the gut, in the groin, changes our internal chemistry, even as it challenges or teases the mind. Good poetry pushes the boundaries of what we know, or thought we knew. Volumes of poetry are seldom best-sellers, and poets seldom grow rich from their books, but, as William Carlos Williams has said, people "die miserably every day / for lack of what is found" in poems.

Poetry provides me a way of waking in the morning to mystery, to a kind of harmony I do not experience otherwise. It offers a way of seeing beyond the superficial, of making startling connections. It allows a way of living deeply, intensely, a way of living in the moment, of being fully awake, aware, of being mindful.

Given the demands of living and teaching, I had been reluctant to engage in any project that would keep poetry from informing my life, that would keep me from my primary passion. But when I began these essays in April 2001, Steve and I had recently returned from Fulbright professorships in Bulgaria and were still on leave from the University of Texas at San Antonio. I had wrapped up several other projects in the works, and found myself suddenly eager to accept patient Ed's long-standing offer.

Throughout the early stages of writing these essays, I had to quiet the voice within me that said, "Who on earth cares how you wrote this poem?" But finally that voice quieted. Writing these short prose pieces has taught me more about my own poetic process than has any other experience. For the first time in over twenty years, I went back over old work to see what it was that engendered poems. For the first time, I attempted to explain the process of writing a poem.

I was finding what fed me as an artist; I was affirming what in my writing life worked. Some of what I learned came as no surprise: I need an enormous amount of solitary time. Like Thoreau, "I love a broad margin to my life." In striving for "Simplicity, simplicity, simplicity," in the midst of our culture's Saint Vitus' dance, living as we do at a faster pace than the author of *Walden* could have imagined, I seldom lunch or shop with friends or party on weekends. I remember what my son David said, when in the fourth grade and overwhelmed with homework: "I never have time to think anymore." I was that child too, always fighting for time to think, mull, and evaluate and to create aesthetic patterns from my perceptions and experiences.

But solitude, as many of these essays emphasize, is not enough. I have long known how much I need writerly friends. In writing *Poems' Progress* I have realized just how essential others have been. Without friends to read drafts, to encourage, to make suggestions, often I would not have had the internal strength to continue. These essays are, at least in part, a way of paying tribute to the mentors, friends, and family members who have helped along the way.

And for those who have helped, with the poems and with the life, I am profoundly thankful. Even if I tried to name everyone, I would still be leaving someone out. Many students have helped over the years, sometimes when they may not even have known it. I remember one young man walking into my office and making an observation about Helen of Troy that sparked a whole series of poems. Students' reactions and suggestions in workshops have been invaluable. I am particularly grateful to my graduate students over the years. To writers who generously have helped with drafts: Kevin Clark, David Dooley, James Hathaway, Paulette Jiles, Catherine Kasper, Doran Larson, Christine Dumaine Leche, Denise Levertov, Pat Mora, Walt McDonald, Naomi Shihab Nye, Alicia Ostriker, Heather Sellers, Hannah Stein, and Diane Wakoski, I am most grateful.

I am thankful for the publishers of my collections of poems: David Bowen, Joseph Bruchac, Bryce Milligan, and Sudeep Sen. I am lucky to have had Ed Wilson as editor and publisher for this volume; his encouragement, expertise, suggestions, and flexibility have all contributed to the pleasure of writing this book. To my former husband Laurence Barker, who willingly dropped the sports pages of the *San Francisco Chronicle* and later the *San Antonio Express-News* to read yet another draft, I express gratitude. I am deeply grateful to Sandra M. Gilbert and Ruth Stone, poetry paragons and mentors extraordinaire, who have mothered my poems from the days when, barely over thirty, I "came out" of the poetry closet. For the sustaining friendship of colleagues Brenda Claiborne and Bonnie Lyons, I am thankful. I am profoundly grateful for the committed presence in my life of Beverly Davis. I am greatly indebted to the group of women who have gathered regularly since 1987, including Vera Banner, Cyra Dumitru, Melissa Shepherd, Veda Smith, and Barbara Stanush, as well as Sharon Godbey and Sherry McKinney, who, in differing ways and at different times, have provided friendship of the deepest kind. For the continuing counsel and inspiration of Jeannine Keenan, central figure in this group of talented women, I cannot adequately express my gratitude.

Most of all, I am grateful to my patient, insightful, and brilliant partner. Steve edited each of these essays as it was written and, finally, read through the entire manuscript, taking hours of time away from his own writing. My gratitude can only be expressed as the days go on between us. "Days," Steve is fond of saying, quoting from Philip Larkin, "are where we live." Perhaps as we continue to live in them he will come to know what he gives.

And finally, it is my son David to whom I dedicate this book. A gifted artist now himself, David often received less-than-ideal mothering because I was immersed in my own art, in graduate school, or in teaching. He is well on his way as a successful musician. If this book can help strengthen his already firm commitment to music and to his own growth, if it can remind anyone that writing, or making art, is a long process of leisure and labor, rapture and rupture, pleasure and pain—of life lived, that is—then perhaps it will have some value beyond my self-indulgent delight in discovering how my poems have progressed.

W. B.

❖ CONTENTS ❖

❖ PRACTICE ❖

PRACTICE

Honing   I'm
Sharpening   my
Knives   for
Cutting   cleaving through
Greenpeppers   opening their
Halves   crackle moist
Dark   white feathers tiny
Seeds   clinging.

This green
meat   will make
good eating   I
will swallow   the seeds
and grow   wings.

About the Writing

S uch a little poem. Yet it was a milestone for me. "Practice" was the first poem I ever wrote intentionally, conscious I was writing a poem, and determined to finish. But I had been writing, for the sheer joy of it, since I was five.

I started writing shortly after learning to write my name, which at first I wrote as "Wendy Bendy," since my mother answered the phone right after showing me how to draw the B, and I just kept going. Soon I was writing letters to my grandparents in New Jersey and to my granny in England. I kept voluminous diaries. As a teenager, I wrote a poem together with my mother, for an optional history assignment. We used Lewis Carroll's verse that begins, "Tweedledum and Tweedledee agreed to have a battle" to parody a political argument between Andrew Jackson and John Quincy Adams. Since my British mother knew nothing about United States history, and since I was mainly delighted to be doing something besides dishes with my mother, the poem received a B-, a low grade for me.

No English teacher ever assigned writing a poem in any class I took. We had no poets in the schools. But when I began teaching high school English, and students began bringing me their tentative poems, I wanted to support them, help them gain confidence. And in encouraging them, I encouraged myself. I began filling the little pads high school teachers use (pink for absence forms, green for tardies, yellow for hall passes) with observations, phrases, and descriptions. I never typed them, or worked on them, I just put them in a drawer. By the time I wrote "Practice," several drawers were so full I could barely open them. I had begun to realize that, although I devoured short stories and novels, it was not the elements of fiction, of character development and plot, that most excited me. It was poetry.

The first stanza of "Practice" came full-born, whole, in a rush. It was the kind of experience a writer longs for. Whoosh, and it's there, the Muse, the breezes, whatever force it is, it's with you. That March of 1975 I was three-months pregnant, a fearful, eager, thirty-two-year-old doctoral student at the University of California at Davis. I had finally left high school teaching, having realized if I were ever going to do what I wanted to in life—study and teach literature *(and write)*—I had better get started. I had come to U.C. Davis with a stellar M.A. record from Arizona State University, but on my arrival at Davis, I failed the English Department's "prelim" exam, a shattering experience. Now I had another chance. If I failed, my fallback position was to enroll in library science. At least I could help get people to books, I reasoned. But I was determined not to fail again.

I sought out advice from faculty. I studied with a friend. I studied on my own. And I found the reading and note-taking exhilarating. Even though I had recently been preparing for Arizona State's M.A. exam, this was different: whereas before, I concentrated primarily on nineteenth- and twentieth-century American literature, now I needed to fill a number of specific literary gaps, particularly poets, from John Donne to Theodore Roethke. I practiced writing *explications de textes*. I read more poetry more attentively than I ever had before.

And I began to realize that my own writings looked like poems. It was word play, sound play, rhythm, imagery that characterized my jottings. I *thought* in lines. I had been writing poems, for years, and had not admitted it. Finally, I let the cat out of the hat, let my secret out. "Practice" was my coming out of the closet, as much to myself as to anyone else.

It is the sort of poem that a former student would have labeled "one of Wendy's kitchen poems." But I was not in the kitchen cutting up peppers when the first stanza came. It arrived because I became intrigued by the word "honing," which means "sharpening," and which, to my delight, I realized, rhymes with "droning," a word for "drudgery." "Honing" sounds also like "homing," which means to return home, and I was, in effect, myself coming home—to my passion for reading and writing, to a full commitment to the life that, from girlhood, I had wanted to lead.

Poems had always made me so excited I could not read them before going to sleep. As a child I read novels under the covers with a flashlight; but once I put the book down, my mind didn't whirr and buzz—I could fall asleep. Reading poetry gave me the shivers, made "my whole body" feel, as Emily Dickinson put it, "so cold no fire ever can warm me." And when, after dinner, my father stood up from his armchair, putting down his watery bourbon to pick up a battered copy of Frost, or Keats, or Shakespeare, and read lines out loud to me, saying, with tears in his voice, "Isn't that beautiful?" I would be so moved I could not speak. In rare moments of familial playfulness, my parents would recite poems together over dinner, one remembering a pair of lines, the other the next. When I began teaching high school English, in my early twenties, it was poetry I most loved—reading poems aloud, conducting discussions with students. Like petals of water lilies, the lines opened their intricacies.

But that same father who read poetry to me, who fed me books—novels, plays, poems—all through my childhood and teens, shattered me when he responded to my telling him, at nineteen, that I knew I wanted to write, that my professors had said I was gifted, by scoffing (after his third or fourth bourbon and soda), "You? What would you have to say?" This was the same father who had told me I could not accept the scholarships I had won to the Eastern colleges I was burning to attend; flights, clothes, other expenses would mean a hardship for the family, he reasoned, and since I was a girl, and would only be marrying and having children soon anyway, I would be a "bad investment." By the time I wrote "Practice," fifteen years had passed since I left high school for the University of Arizona. Thirteen years had passed since I put away any hopes of serious writing, carrying out part of my father's cynical prediction and marrying.

No wonder the second stanza was a nightmare to write. It seemed as though the Muses had flown into the craters on the dark side of the moon. What did I have to say, anyway? I tried several possibilities, the first being:

> Razor sharp   I'm
> Penetrating   surfaces
> Seeing through
> Wholes   into parts
> Endings into
> Beginning.

This, of course, articulates what I was doing at thirty-two: turning something that had ended into a new beginning. But I knew the stanza was not strong enough. I tried this:

> Clean bladed   tearless
> I slice into   slippery onions
> Finding   interlocking rounds
> Firm patterns   crisp for
> Strong eating.

I knew these images were clearer than in the earlier ending, but I also realized these lines were not as interesting as the poem's first stanza. I was stuck. Nevertheless, I kept the poem, with the two unfinished second stanzas, and began writing more poems. It seemed the more I read and studied, the more I wrote.

My son was born by Caesarean section five months after I started "Practice." I had passed the prelim. Our prematurely born baby grew rapidly, and my course work went well. Some time in his second year, my third year at Davis, I grew brave enough to show a group of poems to Sandra Gilbert, who at that time, early in her career, had just begun collaborating with Susan Gubar on *The Madwoman in the Attic.* I know I shook, at least inwardly, as I handed poems to her. But she liked them. She took them seriously. She seemed delighted by what I had to say. She urged me to publish them. But she also made it clear that "Practice" needed more attention, more work. Specifically, it needed another second stanza.

What I realize now is that the poem was especially difficult to finish because I was not allowing the poem to develop its own metaphoric logic. The first stanza had come because I was simply playing around with words; the second stanza would not come because I was trying to say something too consciously and superficially. When I returned to the image of the green pepper, its crisp flesh, the "white feathers" and seeds, the poem found its own ending. And in writing that I would grow wings, I pushed through a kind of mental barrier, opened myself to new levels of possibility. Amazing! Me? Fly? Well, I wanted to, didn't I?

I never put this poem in a book. I am glad I can now, although I am struck by its hesitancy, by the separations between words and phrases, as if I were still not confident of what I was saying. Very few poems I have written use white space in this way. "Practice" was my first accepted poem. In June of 1977, Elliot Gilbert, whom at the time I knew only as Davis's leonine Victorianist and graduate advisor, took it for the *California Quarterly,* which he edited. By the time it appeared in the summer of 1978, my son was a sturdy three-year-old, and the Gilberts had become not only mentors but family friends—neighbors, it turned out, of ours in Berkeley. Later Elliot would joke about "Practice," calling it my "C-section poem." What he may not have realized is that he was right: it is a poem about a birth, but about my own. And what he never knew, before he died in 1991, is that he and especially Sandra were not only midwives to the poem and to all that followed, but were also parents for me, in the best sense of the word. Not that many years older than I, they encouraged, supported, and criticized, always with amazing confidence that I would come through. It was as if they provided ripe green peppers and a sharp knife, smiled benevolently, and said, "good eating, and go ahead, while you're at it, grow yourself wings."

❖ PERSEPHONE'S VERSION ❖

PERSEPHONE'S VERSION

My mother never
understood how, after that first time
(when the earth cracked and the blackness,
like a magnet,

dragged my feet down to the ore)
how after that, I went by myself, how
every October the pears rotting on the ground
blocked the way down, how

I burrowed under the brown fruit,
found my way, tunneling through loam
past bedrock, drawing nearer and nearer
to the fire. In the light of flame

veins of silver, clots of gold
fed my eyes,
my hands glowed scarlet
as I held them toward the hearth.

I never could explain him to my mother,
how I set up my own forge,
had my own hammer, tongs, built
circlets of rubies, diamonds, topaz.

He didn't nag like Apollo,
always saying "Look at me, look
up, look into my eyes when you
speak." I could carve all day.

Neither my mother nor her
brother ever understood
I went because I wanted to,
year after year. They never knew

that was how I was able
to return each April
to find Narcissus, and to feed
my brilliance to the breeze.

About the Writing

Summer of 1976 in Berkeley, California, the summer of a year of drought so severe we reused water every chance we could, watered the house plants with left-over bathroom basin water. Eventually they died; soap scum does not feed a ficus. Our son was not yet a year, still in diapers, and trying to walk, holding up his arms so he could hook his fingers around ours to steady his tottering. I spent as much time bent over as I did standing up.

But not bent over my desk. During the summer I took a break from graduate work. Our budget needed to recover from the cost of child care, and, more important, my son needed some unbroken amounts of time with his mother. His father's vegetable garden flourished, even on gray water. We flushed the toilet once a day. The dirty diapers piled in the hamper. The place reeked.

In July my husband's mother decided it was time to visit. That was her way. She decided; it was time. Once she had unexpectedly arrived on our doorstep and said, "I thought I'd surprise you." She had opinions about everything, especially religion: Methodist, necessary for all good people, and when were we going to find our church home? For years she had asked us when we were going to "start our family" (which postponed our intentions of conception by at least a year every time she asked) and now that our son was trying to toddle into the world, she felt her position as grandmother was God-given and something her son and I had no business meddling with.

She had made the trip from Arizona in her 1963 Dodge with plenty of clothes for a good long visit—oh, three weeks, a month. She liked to be part of our lives. She liked to help my husband with his gardening. She did not like to sweep the kitchen floor, or wash dishes, or dry them, or fold laundry. Every woman has her own method, she would say. Occasionally she asked if she could help me out, and I would say, yes, thanks, could you dry the dishes? But then she would fall silent over her crossword puzzle and that would be that. She loved helping my husband can tomatoes and peaches. I washed the pots and pans with as little water as I could.

She had been with us for about two weeks when this poem came. One day I had driven out to U.C. Davis, my haven, my graduate school. During the summer my mind had gone numb. I was a toddler's walking machine, a kitchen drudge, a water-saver, a diaper-doer. My husband was drunk by six in the evening, and his mother talked from the time she woke in the morning at seven. I was spoiling her grandson, she said, as play-by-play she relived out loud her childhood in Kansas. Some of the stories were fascinating. Some of the time. The first time I heard them.

Out at Davis, midsummer, the grass of the quad stretched as if following the earth's curve. I was early to meet my friend. Waiting for her on the grass, I wrote what became "Persephone's Version." I wrote it out of anger. Of course Persephone wanted to burrow underground. Winter was the best time. Away from all that harvesting, that canning of peaches, Demeter's busy-ness, Ceres' earthiness, her insistence on bodily functions, her maternal intrusions. Away from summer visitors. Down there in the dark she could write, could think, could have some peace. Demeter, Ceres, that mother should just give up the search, get on with her life, do all that harvesting herself.

Years later, the poet Ruth Stone said to me, "It's a poem about your husband and your own mother, isn't it?" She was right. My mother disliked my husband, never could understand why I married him. Now, twenty-four years later and divorced, I'm more sympathetic to my mother's viewpoint. But much of the time during those years, like the Hades of "Persephone's Version," my husband did try to give me space, did not ask why I had to write, helped me carve out time for writing, let me alone. And as the years went by, he even began to tell his mother when it was not a good time to visit.

But I am also thinking the poem may have enabled me to express my own fear, even terror, that to carve out poems, to make that descent into the dark underworld of the subconscious, into what Yeats called the "foul rag and bone shop of the heart," is to be seen by those "getting and spending" in the world of surfaces, like living in hell. Doesn't everyone want to spend the summer canning tomatoes and making and eating peach pie? Actually, someone so selfish that what she most wants to do is write must be "bad." To be Persephone, to be "married" or joined to a force that rules underground (subconscious, creative) life, is to be yoked to Hades, to Satan, to the devil himself. In writing the poem, I was facing an internal conflict it has taken years to overcome. In the poem I affirmed myself as a writer, and if my mother, mother-in-law, relatives, and friends saw me as evading responsibilities, as seduced by the devil, then they would just have to deal with it.

Hardest of all has been to deal with the part of myself that likes canning tomatoes, eating blueberry pie, and listening to the stories of people who grew up in Kansas—or Texas—in the twenties. Hardest of all has been learning to negotiate easily back and forth between that underground world of silence and shadows and poems and art, and the world of the people I love.

My son learned to walk. Today, as an artist—a musician, a composer—he regularly makes the descent too, and I leave him alone.

❖ SCHÖNBRUNN YELLOW ❖

SCHÖNBRUNN YELLOW

The summer palace of the Hapsburgs is yellow
and inside, gilt climbs the walls like ivy.

Maria Theresa had sixteen children in this house.
To keep them she had 400 maids.

The yellow walls are the color
of the woman's apron in Brueghel's painting,

a woman dancing on village dirt,
dancing in an apron thick with grease,

an apron hard with scraps of dough.
Maria Theresa's favorite painting

was of three peasants, a family taking a walk in the hills,
a family of peasants like Brueghel's, dancing

and drinking, filling their cheeks with cereal
and beer the color of gold.

About the Writing

Our son was not yet five, and my husband was leading a summer concert tour with the choir and chamber orchestra he directed at Berkeley High. It was an especially ambitious trip: three buses filled with seventy-five high school kids, two chaperones, and the three of us. The students performed in several major cities in Europe, including Prague, Munich, and Vienna.

We had been traveling for two weeks by the time we checked into the hotel in Vienna. Our first morning there, we made the trip out to Empress Maria Theresa's summer palace of Schönbrunn, where we joined crowds so thick I was afraid our child would be crushed if we did not carry him. Part of a river of tourist sludge, we trudged at a funereal largo through miles of roped-off rococo bric-a-brac. Impossible to move at your own pace, pause over a particular vase, or hustle through a room when you had seen enough.

I felt far more impatient and claustrophobic than our son, who had plenty of attention from the tenors and baritones who good-humoredly took turns riding him on their sturdy shoulders, high above crowd level. I wished someone would carry me. I felt as I did after football games, which I never wanted to attend in the first place, but could endure as long as everyone was sitting down. Once a game was over and thousands of people began all at once heading for their cars, I wanted out, and fast. People used to tease me, saying I was a born quarterback, referring to the way I could slip through and out of a crowd.

I could not get away from that palace fast enough. The first time I had seen Versailles I understood the reasons for the French Revolution, and here I had that sort of reaction again. Maybe it was because we were traveling on a strict budget and many of the students had more money to spend than we did. (We carefully budgeted our coffees, our ice creams, the little toys we picked up to keep our boy entertained during eight- and ten-hour bus trips.) Maybe it was because we found Vienna such an expensive city we could barely afford to buy any of the cake for which it was so famous. For whatever reasons, I had no patience with this architectural concoction and its outrageous excesses, or with the hordes of people who wanted to gawk.

In the afternoon, after our buses had brought us back into Vienna, and after a good lunch, we walked to the Kunsthistorisches Museum, whose cool gray halls were sprinkled with art enthusiasts (the swarms of other tourists, I assumed, were off downing elaborate cakes and expensive coffees). I breathed deeply and set out to find the Brueghels.

I had wanted to see Brueghel's paintings since first reading William Carlos Williams' poem "The Dance," where "the dancers go round, they go round and / around," their "hips and their bellies off balance / to turn them." I knew the picture on which the poem was based, *The Kermess,* or *The Wedding Dance,* was not here. But other Brueghels were. I found them easily, on the first floor. There was no one else in the room. I sat down on a broad wooden bench, spellbound, especially by *The Peasant Dance.* Even though I knew Brueghel's vision of humanity was grim, even though I knew he had painted these faces to represent disagreeable, quarreling, foolish people, I felt in these canvases an enormous vitality. Here, after a stifling morning, was life.

Here were solid swaths of the colors of blood and muscle, earth and stone. So what if the church faded into the background? So what if the man in the foreground looked grimacing, even brutal? Brueghel probably intended me to react very differently from the way I did, which was with relief, with a sense of kinship to the foregrounded yellow-aproned woman, with a sense of my own blood flowing through my body, my own rhythms returning. I sat and looked and looked, and then brought out my notebook and wrote the poem, almost as it appears here.

Now, years later, I think the poem was a way of saying I was glad to be who I was, to be part of our little imperfect family, financially strapped though we were. I did not want to be walled in by the trappings of royalty, by rules that kept me bound to the constraints of courtly values and manners that would decree, for instance, that I could not have suckled my own baby, would have had to bring in a wet nurse. Of course, I romanticized the poverty and ignorance shown in Brueghel's painting. But I was expressing my own pleasure in life lived, life felt, danced with two feet thumping the ground, expressing my delight in laughing, tickling my child, hugging my husband with his big pot-belly. It was a poem of affirmation.

And I had a hunch the Empress Maria Theresa—who reportedly cradled her infant son in her arms on at least one occasion while appearing in her official capacity—would have understood.

❖ ONE LEMON ❖

ONE LEMON

Still house after rain in the night,
small sun drops over the floor.

On the wood table
one lemon, fine-grained,

two daffodils, still dripping
from the garden, still too wet

for the water to pearl.
Stems green-lined like thin veneer.

One lemon. Daffodils, the yellow
that's been missing

all winter. Even the chickens
had stopped laying, we had

to use market eggs, pale yolks.
The smell of these flowers

is from another earth.
Cut open the lemon, squeeze

and stir in honey,
maybe heal a sore throat.

ARRANGEMENTS

On the clean wood
table one lemon,
two yellow daffodils,
lemon at an angle
with the long green stems,
perfect still-life.
No film.
The flowers drip from last
night's rain, one petal
is folded under
the rest of the flower.
Move it,
so it won't bruise.
Fill the vase with water.
~~Black glass from Venice.~~
Pinch off the stems,
they're too tall for the glass.
Pinch off more.
Need some leaves.
Flower heads won't hold
up by themselves.
Go outside, ~~had this~~
~~morning,~~ pick leaves,
fine-grained as the maple
of the ~~cutting~~ table.
The leaves hold up the flowers
a bit better.
No. Need one more daffodil
for balance.
The lemon rolls onto the floor.
Pick it up, cut it in two.
Squeeze the halves dry.
Soft ~~Empty~~ yellow shells go the hens.
The wood table is left
with half a dozen drops
of water and one
~~and one~~ lemon seed.

36

Feb. 1981

About the Writing

After September 11, 2001, and with terrorist-suicide mass murders continuing in the Middle East as I write, the world seems even more frightening, dangerous, and overwhelming than it did twenty years ago, when this simple poem was written. First drafted in February, 1981, it began as a much longer poem, yet from the beginning it expressed a need for simplicity in the midst of life often overwhelming in its complexity.

Our family's kitchen was all white, with deep blue-green ceramic tiles and butcher block tables. It faced southwest, with windows on both sides, so even on Berkeley's foggy days it was light. Normally, dozens of dirty pots and pans cluttered the counters; my former husband, an obsessive cook, was constantly trying out new and complex recipes. Sauces bubbled and splattered up to the ceiling, and cleaning up was my job. I was writing a dissertation. The kitchen was rarely tidy.

But it was pristine on the morning that occasioned the poem. For some reason even the dishes from the night before had been put away. My husband had picked a ripe lemon from our tree by the front door and left it on the butcher-block table in the center of the kitchen. A little later, I brought in two of the first daffodils from the garden and dropped them on the table before I began looking for a vase. The three yellow objects on the bare wood in the clean white and blue kitchen dazzled me, mesmerized.

The first typed draft of the poem reprinted here shows it took some time to find the poem. Like the usual state of the kitchen itself, the poem began as a cluttered thing. I had a hard time letting the poem be as simple as the moment of its conception. In fact, it was my determination to write out what I was trying to do, which was to make an "arrangement," that almost caused me to lose the poem. In the rewriting, however, I was able to go back to the initial moment of seeing, and focus on that dazzling moment, on the objects themselves.

In *Still Life with Oysters and Lemon*, Mark Doty describes the significance of looking—that we reveal ourselves by how we look, what we look at. He discusses the value of still life as a genre of painting, calling attention to the rich ambiguity of the phrase "still life." In the paintings, the arranged pears, or lemons, apples, or oysters, appear still fresh: they are still filled with life. And yet their preciousness, he notes, lies in their fragility, their temporality. They won't last much longer. Those daffodils would droop and crinkle in a few days, and, even in the refrigerator, the lemon would not last more than a week or two. The scene itself could not last. I had to leave the room to find a vase for the flowers, think about where I would put the vase, and then the lemon would need to be put away in the fruit basket, so the table could be clear for bread-making, or carrot-cutting, or juice-squeezing. Even if I had left the three objects alone on the table for days, the daffodils would have shriveled. Eventually, so would the lemon. If I could have painted, or photographed that "still life," I would have. Instead, I tried to write a poem.

I am not sure why I did not include "One Lemon" in my first collection, *Winter Chickens*. It belongs in that book: another poem from that garden, that kitchen, when our son was little. Maybe I left it out because even now, I feel the poem is not finished, and want to tinker with it, make it a stronger poem. If I could rewrite it now, I would drop "still" in lines 5 and 6. In line 5, I would replace "two" with "and." I would omit "green" and "thin" in line 8. I would cut "the" on line 9 and drop "yellow" down to line 10, cutting "that's been." I would delete "Even" in line 11 and "we had / to use" in lines 12 and 13. I would change line 13 to read: "market eggs' yolks were pale." In line 15, I would replace "is" with "rises." Then I would delete "open" in line 16, insert a comma after "squeeze," insert a period after "honey" in line 17, and omit "maybe" in the last line. The poem would then read like this:

Still house after rain in the night,
small sun drops over the floor.

On the wood table
one lemon, fine-grained,

and daffodils, dripping
from the garden, too wet

for the water to pearl.
Stems lined like veneer.

One lemon. Daffodils,
yellow missing

all winter. The chickens
had stopped laying,

market eggs' yolks were pale.
The smell of these flowers

rises from another earth.
Cut the lemon, squeeze,

and stir in honey.
Heal a sore throat.

    Even with these changes, I am not satisfied with the poem. But I know I was right in my early decision to use couplets; this poem needs that slower pace, that attention to each line that couplets allow. I like the way even in the first draft included here I crossed out "mad this / morning," which is barely visible now underneath my dark pencil lines. I like the way I found, later, to suggest the depression or anger by saying the yellow had been "missing / all winter," that "Even the chickens / had stopped laying." If chickens do not lay, we know something is wrong.

    Maybe I am not happy with "One Lemon" because, like a sculpture that contains some jagged bits of rock the sculptor has not yet smoothed away, the poem is still more than it needs to be, and therefore does less than it might. I want to reduce it further, and take part of the first line for the title:

AFTER RAIN IN THE NIGHT

one lemon and
two daffodils, resting

on the clean table.
Squeeze the lemon,

drop the blossom
stem in water—more

than honey, these
heal a throat.

I like cutting "sore" from the last line. We automatically think of a sore throat after reading of honey and lemon, and without the word "sore," the line suggests more than physical malaise. I like the off-rhyme of "lemon" and "blossom" and the assonance of "clean," "squeeze," "these," and "heal." I like the way the poem contains a long *o* sound only at the very end in the word "throat," which follows all those *ee* sounds made with the back of our throat kept tight, so that when we come to the *oh* of "throat," we open our throats. In this way the reader, I think, can feel the effect of lemon and blossom more viscerally.

But I fear James Fenton's criticism of Wilfred Owen, that he "was slow to abandon a bad poem," can easily apply to me: I do not think "One Lemon" is much of a poem. (And now I am not even sure that the first version I include, the one originally published in *Poet Lore*, is not the strongest after all.)

Yeats once said a poem is never finished, only abandoned. He abandoned some of the great poems of the English language, poems I return to over and over. Most of mine, and this one in particular, seem to remain unsatisfactory. But even so, I like the way I was able here to write about the incidental shrines of our lives, the small sacred spaces we accidentally—or coincidentally—construct, even (or especially) when, as Wordsworth so famously said, "the world is too much with us." I do not remember what was wrong that morning, why I had been angry, or upset. I do not remember what was happening internationally in February, 1981. But I know that, in the midst of "getting and spending," these little moments of focus can heal, and often more than a sore throat. In "A Prayer for My Daughter," after describing a howling storm (which, in 1919, could refer to a storm caused both by weather and by war), Yeats praises the strengthening power of "custom and ceremony," which he equates with "the spreading laurel tree" and the horn of plenty. The storm in my small poem remains outside its borders, only hinted at by the rain and the winter that seem to be over. One lemon and a few daffodils are hardly a cornucopia, or a deep-rooted, spreading tree. But they are not that different from what Yeats was suggesting, since they too are fruit from the earth, reminders of the natural seasons, of the earth beneath our feet.

Yellow: the color we most associate with light. I returned to "One Lemon" this afternoon precisely because, even though my son is grown and living his own fine life, and even though my companion is as tidy as I am, the "roof-levelling" winds of international events threaten, as they do in Yeats's poem. The chaos of the world swirls barely beyond my own home, my neighbor's "hill," and I miss the lemon tree that, reliable as the sun, once bore its yellow fruit by my front door.

❖ FROM THE ATTIC AT THORNFIELD ❖

FROM THE ATTIC AT THORNFIELD

She did not want to burn
down the house because
she was in love with fire.

It was never that.
It was because of the closed
doors, the straight walls

that stopped any long breathing,
that told her, when she tried
to laugh, to stop.

And the chairs, the chairs
slim and delicate,
lined against the edge

of a room, lap sideways
to lap, no one facing.
Even the windows looking out

felt too slick and hard
to her fingers, nothing open
about them. How did she know

that what she saw
outside was really there?
That the hedges were any more

yielding than a locked door?
And the stones rose in walls so high,
so thick, she had never found

the way out.
          In the first delicate
lickings of flame, the lovely

leafings of orange, yellow,
the prickings and twinings
of the snapping noises,

she could hear voices,
the click of new tongues,
the lap of loud breathing,

and she knew
that as the roar began,
with its great wind, blackness,

red over brightest red, flames
that took over the sky,
she knew she did love it

now, it was all
she had ever loved,
this sweet terror

that raced its own body
together with hers
over the terraces, the gardens,

out to the orchards, the hills,
its blazing voice
finally loud enough,

that the only way it would ever stop
would be when it had spoken
to everything it could find,

and there would be,
for the first time,
nothing left, nothing

left to say.

About the Writing

Anger I have always tamped down, like tobacco into the bowl of a pipe. And I resist lighting the pipe, would never smoke it, would rather hand it over to someone else. But maybe it is more like dirt I sweep under a rug, accumulating till I trip, fall, break something. I wrote "From the Attic at Thornfield" in rage. I think it was anger at my own son, perhaps the most unacceptable anger of all for a woman. Anger at your own child? What kind of mother are you? How could you? I do not remember why I was angry. What I remember is feeling fury, and bringing it, for the first time, directly to the computer, to the writing.

But I still could not claim my rage, could not say I was angry. Oh I wrote out the anger all right, but made it belong to someone else. *Jane Eyre* was one of those novels I had read as a teenager that reached my marrow. I knew this story from the inside out, knew it viscerally, even though I did not even visit England until I was twenty-seven, and even though it took graduate school and Sandra Gilbert's first course on women and literature to give me the critical apparatus to describe mad Bertha—who burns down the house—as prim Jane's alter ego. So, like Charlotte Brontë, I could (briefly) let bloated, bestial Bertha carry my anger, and metaphorically at least, let it burn everything in its path. Much safer than saying outright whatever it was I wanted to say.

This is, of course, also a poem about fearing I had so much to say that the only way I could let it out would be cataclysmically destructive. And yet it is, simultaneously, a poem about desiring that release: "and there would be, // for the first time, / nothing left, nothing // left to say." Even now, I feel an almost orgasmic relief in those last lines. If only we could say all that we could. But the line breaks create a double entendre: the line "nothing left, nothing" suggests these "new tongues" would in fact destroy everything that is something in the world. The emphasis is on "nothing." And the poem's last line, "left to say," affirms there will always be, no matter what, something still left to say. It is a quiet irony, but an irony nevertheless.

Looking back over this poem now, I find it a poem very much "on a leash." The triplets create an almost lady-like sense of containment, and yet, at the same time, the poem's rhythms, I think, contribute to building "its blazing voice." Maybe it is this tension that expresses my still-painful ambivalence. To this day I have not written directly about anger. And maybe, in retrospect, at that moment, I did actually want to burn down that particular house.

❖ WASHING IN CREMONA ❖
AT TEN O'CLOCK

WASHING IN CREMONA AT TEN O'CLOCK

Water runs into the sink
over crumpled shirts and socks,
splashes like water falling

on rocks in the mountains
high over grape-vined hills
the green of new peas.

Wring the socks, twist them hard
until they're furrowed as trees.
Hang the shirts in the window.

Water falls through the sleeves,
down the length of the cloth,
small rain on the window sill.

Warm breath of air
carries kitchen clatter,
women's laughter

over the cobbles, lulls
you to dream of clean
clothes that fit like new skin.

About the Writing

Summer concert tours with the Berkeley High School choir and chamber orchestra were thrilling; the students received ovations from local audiences everywhere they performed. But we spent only one or two days in each city on the itinerary, fitting in sightseeing tours, rehearsals, and meals before the students' evening concerts. With our mornings, noons, and evenings spent on guided tours, in cafeteria-style restaurants, and concert halls—or on buses for anywhere from six to twelve hours between cities—I often found it difficult to maintain my balance, my composure, my energy—my self. There was no "down" time (the thinking was, you had to keep high school kids busy, or who knows what they might do), no free hours to saunter off, away from noise and banter. And stuck in rush-hour traffic on the bus filled with high school singers and musicians, my toddler son in my lap, my choral-director husband in the front seat next to the chain-smoking German bus driver, with our bus leading two other buses each filled with students and a chaperone, I wanted out.

I jumped at the chance, late in the evening, to bring our son back to the hotel room and put him to bed. I shut out street noise by closing the shutters. My boy and I could spread out, unpack a little. He could play on the floor while I did laundry by hand in the bathroom basin. Rinsing Woolite from my son's small shirts, I relished the sound of the cool water, not unlike the sounds of water falling on rocks of a stream, on the leaves of trees lining the mountains that lifted beyond the cities we visited. As I hung our family's socks in the windowsill, I let my mind wander and float, as if I could clean my inner self just as I cleaned the clothes, wringing out the dirty water, the excess, so the next morning, once again, I could start fresh.

I wrote "Washing in Cremona at Ten O'Clock" in that northern Italian town after hanging up our family's socks, shorts, and shirts over the towel rails, the shower head, door knobs, and the window sill. Both my little son and my large husband had fallen asleep, and for the first moment since waking that morning, I was alone. I responded by turning on my travel light and jotting a draft of this poem in my journal. I should have been sleeping; we had to be up at six for another long day on the bus. But even more than sleep, I needed some time in my own mind, a respite from the tension and chatter of the day.

I have always liked Cremona, and not only because it was the first

Italian town I had ever visited, long before our son was born. In January of 1972, we arrived at two in the morning in dense winter fog, my husband feverish with an ear infection. The next morning I followed three kindly women in black dresses who energetically gestured me to the nearest *farmacia*. We stayed a week, and not only because my husband was ill.

Cremona is a vital market town, filled not with tourists but with local people going about the business of their lives. I like the spaciousness of the Piazza del Duomo, the sense that this is a city center so filled with its own life that visitors are incidental. Daily life continues here, it seems, uninterrupted by those of us who drop in from elsewhere. That night, the only one awake in our room, I heard through the shutters the voices of women across the alley talking and laughing amid the clatter of washing dishes.

Maybe washing our clothes in the basin made me feel a kinship with these women going about their daily (and nightly) lives, doing their housework. Strange though it sounds, when I travel I often miss the physical tasks of ordinary life. I actually like doing laundry in the basin at night. I can recover from social and sensory overload by washing out my own clothes, by giving my hands something simple and repetitive to do, focus for just a few minutes on something I know well, on the layers that clothe the skin. It helps me remember who I am. I sleep more soundly.

Writing "Washing in Cremona at Ten O'Clock" was a way to protect and preserve just such a moment of respite, a simple act of familiar dailiness that sustained, refreshed, and renewed. In the midst of that grueling trip, it gave me space.

❖ EXORCISM OF A NIGHTMARE ❖

EXORCISM OF A NIGHTMARE

I sit on the bed, warm under blankets, and
there you are
on the chair facing me, probing,

"Why no poems these days?
Actually none of them are any good,
just more fifth-rate clutter

robbing the woods of their bones again.
Why not let the child use the paper
for his charming drawings?

Why not his father? The paper would help
start the fire, cold mornings."
But I'm eating my words.

One day my mouth will open and the words
will roll out, thousands of miles
of scrolls with red lettering

and the air will fill
with words like Chinese kites
surging and dipping in the air,

dances even a child can read,
and we, lightened, will quite simply
walk across the street to King Tsin,

sit at the windows, order squid and ginger beef,
laughing at the leaping of the kites,
at the scrolls of silver flying in blue air.

EXORCISM OF A NIGHTMARE

I sit on the bed, warm under blankets, and
there you are
on the chair facing me, probing,

"Why no poems these days?
Actually none of them are any good,
just more fifth-rate clutter

robbing the woods of their bones again.
Why not let the child use the paper
for his charming drawings?

Why not his father? The paper would help
start the fire, cold mornings."
But I'm eating ~~paper~~ *my words*

~~Swallowing it down in small wet bits.~~
~~I'll digest it all~~
~~Not instantly. Probably not for years~~
One day *will*
~~will~~ my mouth, open and ~~the paper will~~ *the will*
roll out, thousands of miles
of scrolls with red lettering.

~~Out my mouth the words will unfurl~~
~~like the tongues of lilies~~
~~and my words will unfurl~~ *cut*

~~so you look inside yourself,~~
~~swallow my words into yourself,~~
~~digest them, roll out your own after awhile.~~

Then the air will fill
with ~~our~~ words like Chinese kites
surging and dipping in the air,

dances even a child can read,
and we, lightened, will quite simply
walk across the street to eat,

sit at the windows, order squid and ginger beef,
laughing at the leaping of the kites,
at the scrolls of silver flying in blue air.

Fall 1980

About the Writing

This may be the only time I have ever written a poem directly about a real nightmare. My shoulders still contract from the fear generated by this dream, by its caustic speaker. By the fall of 1980, immersed in graduate studies at the University of California at Davis, I found it hard to make time for writing poetry. By this time, I had developed a modest record: I had published fourteen poems in little magazines. I wrote in the corners and crannies of my life, often late at night, and often jotting lines for poems on the hour-long twice-weekly commute from Berkeley to Davis. (This was dangerous, although perhaps not as risky as using a cell phone while driving: I would move into the middle lane of the interstate, assume a moderate speed, and balance a note pad on the steering wheel.) But from the time I "came out" and openly committed myself to writing poems, I found I was happiest, most balanced, when I was drafting or revising poems. The trouble was, seminars in Henry James or Nathaniel Hawthorne did not benefit from my scrawlings and meditations on green peppers or laundry, and I needed to finish my Ph.D. and find a job.

The nightmare came during a period of little poetry. Early in the fall quarter, I had begun my dissertation on Emily Dickinson and was overwhelmed by the project's scope. My son had entered kindergarten, but kindergarten lasted only from 9:00 to 11:30 in the morning, and nursery school afterward proved exhausting for him. So I walked him to school after breakfast, and returned to walk him home again for a quiet lunch and a less structured afternoon. I had two hours every weekday morning to work on Dickinson.

The poem reports the dream verbatim. Who the questioner in the nightmare was, I do not know. But, obviously, it represented that part of me who criticizes everything I undertake for my own growth. And also obviously, this internal critic was urging me to give up writing, let my son and his father make use of the "paper" or any resources I was wasting by . trying to write "fifth-rate" poems that would only "clutter" the landscape and "rob the woods of their bones." By attempting to write poems, I was, the dream's speaker warned, harming not only my family but also the environment, and for a worthless cause.

Composing the poem was an exorcism. I began by writing down the nightmare's questions verbatim, determined I would answer back. I quelled my own doubts as I wrote, devouring or destroying the words of the dream, while simultaneously affirming that, once digested, once fully part of me, language would emerge like those stunning, silvery Chinese kites, and our family would go out together to the best Northern Chinese restaurant we knew, and laugh over a luxurious dinner, exhilarated at our new freedom resulting from the words' release. And maybe the ecstatic tone of the poem's ending comes from a sense that my words could result in a celebration not only benefiting all the members of my family, but also involving my nasty internal critic, who could join me, transformed. Perhaps writing could result in uniting the conflicting sides of myself.

The draft I include here is an early one I took to Sandra Gilbert for suggestions. It was she who suggested the clever double entendre, "But I'm eating my words," the poem's pivotal line. And typically, she wisely urged "a little judicious pruning," as she used to say, which was exactly what the poem needed. The draft shows Sandra's pencilled suggestions.

After working further on the poem, at Sandra's urging, I sent the poem to John Nims, at that time the editor of *Poetry*. I mailed him "Exorcism of a Nightmare" on February 18, 1981; ten days later, he accepted it. Ecstatic, I called Sandra, and wrote a spate of joyful (and terrible) poems about the energizing effects of acceptance letters.

I wish I could say since "Exorcism of a Nightmare" I have never suffered through a period of such self-doubt, of feeling that I will never write a poem again, or that nothing I have written is any good. But it seems to be a Slough of Despond into which I frequently descend. Recently, while writing one of these essays, I whined to my companion, "Maybe I'll never be able to write poems again." He reminded me I had written a decent poem the week before. I grumped and moaned. The next day I drafted a new poem.

Once I took some of my early poems to Ruth Stone, now eighty-six, one of the most brilliant American poets writing today and a most valued muse, model, and mentor. I asked her if they were any good. She looked at me (and Ruth looks not only straight at you, but straight through you) and asked: "Can you stop?"

❖ FOR WANT OF DOLLS ❖

The Poem

FOR WANT OF DOLLS

1.
A woman bends
over a blanket she opens
to offer a gift: Peruvian

dolls for the dead.
Formed from shreds, figures shaped
like family, friends, made

to keep the dead from loneliness.
Their yarn mouths grin
wide ovals, loose braids drift

down long skirts, the weave
ravelling, threads dropped
from the warp.

Some of the dolls hold
little ones, babies, faces
pale as the shells of eggs.

One lies on her back, swollen belly
covered with a tapestry of gold, red.
Three figures lean over her

as the baby emerges.
I gather the dolls in a row
in my room. Silent

color of berries,
doves, of rings
inside trees.

2.
Six years old, Phoenix
subdivision too new for trees,
too hot for flowers, I craved

the Story Book Dolls at the dime store,
full skirts that rustled
like petals pressed

into cardboard and cellophane boxes.
Dolls named after stories I read
in my room with the blinds

drawn from the sun, from the square yard
outside, bare except for the oleander,
castor beans we were told

never to touch with our mouths.
I saved my nickels
for months, but all I could buy

was a plain doll, short skirt,
not someone from a book,
Snow White, Sleeping

Beauty cost too much, their velvet
and lace, coiled hair, shining
crowns. I wanted them

to bloom in a row over my bed,
their wide skirts, petticoats
ruffling the bare wall.

3.
I remember in France, driving to Chartres,
how the cathedral
lifts the valley around it. I remember

our eyes rising to portals
where saints are gathered
in rows, where stone

has been carved into lace, stories
for people who couldn't read.
And I remember how we entered

in silence the vault of light
and faced the rose
window, its great round

ringing circles within
circles
          where doves wing

down to the mother
offering her child,
pale, oval faces blooming.

THE WOMAN WHO CRAVED DOLLS

(For J.K.)

July 2, 89
alterns

No country for a small
boned girl, fresh from the crisp blue
air of white New Hampshire pine, moss underfoot
thick as the Persian rugs throughout
her grandparents´ house.

Some transplants don´t take.
Only in December, January,
did rows of ranunculus bloom
in her mother´s worked square of yard,
the tiny tubers like claws
that forced up leaves of green lace,
and flowers

                like long dresses,
like Cinderella´s after the fairy
godmother´s wand had worked.

By April in Phoenix it was too hot
for anything to grow, except zinnias
that scratched, and castor
beans that everyone knew
were poison.

[And always the sun.]
The few leaves that struggled on
the mulberry trees cast no shadows.
Only safe in her room with Venetian
blinds could she carve
tunnels that curved down
into shadows, damp earth, and small-
faced violets.

Grandparents, relatives, all back
East or in England, her god-
father dead in Bogota, the one
who had sent her silver, the only one
who could make her father laugh.

Every week she saved her nickel
allowance, planning to collect
story book dolls--the ones all the girls
bought at the dime store
and hung on their walls,
slim dolls with red cheeks,
slim curved arms, their hair

like flowers,
roses, rununculus that could bloom
all year on ~~your walls,~~ petals of silk,
scarlet, velvet, purple, blues, and lace,
pink, violet, ivory, ribbons.
Stories to line. ~~the walls~~
~~of~~ her room:
              Snow White, silent
years under hot glass, and still *became*
queen. Cinderella, every night the dishes,
the kitchen floor, and yet she grew
to live in a palace of spires that winked
in a lavendar sky under the moon.
Heidi, bright embroidery *leaping with white*
bobbing over the Alps, ~~nuzzling milk~~ goats, *blue ribbon,*
And Alice, blond hair long and free *under a*
who explored the tunnels right underneath her feet.

But half a year of saved nickels couldn't even buy one.
All she could buy with her dollar and a half was a young
girl doll, straight short skirt, no flounces,
no laces, a jumper, plaid school dress cut off at the knees.
Not even someone from a book.

2.
January mist, morning
on the Ile de France.
They rise above, long, lean,
in perfectly even rows, the stone
statues of the saints lining
the west wall of Notre Dame.
And by each of the portals
leading the new-
comer into this tunnel of lifted light
its windows like flowers
and arches a garden of supple
stems bending with the sweet
weight of their tassel of bloom.

Our Lady, great flower of Paris,
the saints lining its walls
guarding the doors, facing.

3.
It was her friend who came,
bending over a blanket
that she opened to show
four dolls, a gift from Peru,
her daughter's home.
Four dolls, with their babies,
and one more of a woman in childbirth,
a sculpture of rags and woven

2

cloth, the mother surrounded
by three friends, and visible
the head of the baby.

Forty years after all
her nickels didn't
add up to enough.
Peruvian dolls of the dead,
here, in her house,
with its leafy shade,
its ceilings high
above the eye, angles
upon angles like the places
where the branches of trees
meet.

Dolls come from the dead.
Hair loose wool, yarn unwoven
from its cloth so it falls in waves.
Dolls of long lean women, holding
babies at their sides, before them,
babies like little dolls of dolls.
One, the largest, holds out hands
like birds claws wrapped in brown yarn,
her mouth is open, she is telling
stories from under the earth
where she has lived and died
and come to line the walls
of a room that tells stories,
a room where the dolls of the mind
are every day clothed and reclothed.
Hanging in the closet of the next
room are long, soft skirts, wool
and linen, pink, and full.

So when forty years after the story
book dolls were creatures she knew
she could never place on the inside
of her walls, when a small eyes brought
dolls to her house
she knew a garden had opened
right under her own feet.

who brings to her house
with its leafy shade,

THE WOMAN WHO WANTED DOLLS

10/10/89

> O sages standing in God's holy fire
> As in the gold mosaic of a wall,
> Come from the holy fire, perne in a gyre,
> And be the singing-masters of my soul.
> Consume my heart away; sick with desire
> And fastened to a dying animal
> It knows not what it is; and gather me
> Into the artifice of eternity.
>
> --W. B. Yeats

1.
Arizona was no country for a small
boned girl who remembered the blue
air of New Hampshire pines, moss
underfoot thick as the Persian rugs
of her grandparents' house.

Subdivisions too new for trees,
too hot for flowers. Her parents
tried: in the winter they managed
one row of ranunculus, planting in the fall
the tubers, tiny claws that
sent up leaves like old lace, flowers
like long dresses.

But by summer there were only zinnias
that scratched, castor beans that everyone knew
were poison. The leaves that struggled
on the mulberry trees cast no shadows.

She wanted to collect
Story Book Dolls: Snow White, Cinderella,
they would be like flowers
all year for her bedroom wall, their skirts
of lace, velvet, scarlet, blue ribbons.
After half a year of saved nickels
she brought home the only doll she could afford,
a plain girl doll, straight short skirt.
Not even someone from a book.

2.
Twenty years later she saw them, in the early
morning, a cold January mist, the Ile de la Cité:
rising above, lacework in stone, the rows
of statues of saints lining the face

of Notre Dame, stone cloth flowing downward
toward her eyes that lifted, then,
into the vast tunnel of light, its windows
like roses, stories of red ocher, cobalt
blue, and arches like stems bending
with the weight of their tassel, bloom,
great flower of Paris,
rose without end.

3.
So she was ready, when a friend
brought to her house (surrounded by old
green-leaved oaks and grasses
that reddened in autumn) an armful of dolls
like dolls she had never seen: from Peru,
dolls from the dead.

Dolls holding babies--one was five dolls
in one, of a woman in childbirth, the tiny
head of the baby just come through.
The largest of the dolls held out her hands,
claws wrapped in yarn. The cloth
of her long skirt was brown and blue, her hair loose
black wool, the yarns fallen away from the warp,
falling in waves. Her skirt
was striped like the rings of an old tree.
Her mouth opened to a country for old women,
stories, long telling.

ON COLLECTING DOLLS, STORIES TO LIVE WITH

For Jeannine Keenan

11/4/89

1.
Subdivision too new for trees, too hot
for flowers. Six years old, I craved
to collect the Story Book Dolls

they sold at the dime store, dolls
with full skirts that rustled
like petals pressed into cardboard

and cellophane boxes. Dolls
named after stories
I read in my room with the blinds

drawn from the sun, from the square
yard outside where my parents
planted oleander, castor beans that grew fast

but that we knew we must
never touch with our mouths.
I saved my nickels for months, but all

I could afford was a plain doll, with a straight
short skirt. Not even someone
from a book. Snow White, Sleeping

Beauty cost too much, with their velvet
and lace, coiled hair, their shining
crowns. I had wanted them

to line the bare walls
of my room, to hang in rows
over my bed, their skirts

blooming, their mouths
like little cherries
about to burst.

2.
I remember my first time in France,
driving to Chartres, how the cathedral rises
over the valley around it.   I remember

our eyes lifting to the portals where the saints
are gathered in rows, where the stone
has been carved into lace, into stories

for people who didn't read.
And I remember how we entered

in silence the great vault of light

where the windows are jewels held
by ribbons of lead, and I remember
how we faced the western rose.

And later, how we walked down
to the crypt, the earliest remains,
the old, old sacred site.

3.
From Peru, a friend bends over a rough
blanket she opens to offer a gift:
dolls of the dead. Formed

from shreds, the fabric remaining
on figures that had kept
the departed from loneliness.

Their mouths are sewn in yarn wide
open, braids are loose
down the sides of their bodies, long

skirts, the weave ravelling,
threads dropped
from the warp.

Some of the dolls hold
little ones, babies, faces
pale as the eggs of doves.

One lies on her back, swollen
belly covered with a tapestry of gold,
and red. Three figures lean toward her as

the baby emerges. I gather
the dolls in a row
in my room. Silent,

they are the colors of rings
inside trees, ground
doves, ripe berries, and stone.

About the Writing

This is a rare afternoon. I have not talked on the phone to Jeannine Keenan. She and I talked yesterday, for about an hour, and we talked the day before. We see each other only six or seven times a year (we live over an hour apart), but we speak on the phone almost daily. Jeannine is the woman bent over the blanket wrapped around the dolls in the poem. Originally, I had dedicated the poem to her, because the entire meditation sprang from her gift.

She arrived in the midst of a year-end party in full swing. It was May, Friday afternoon, and students were clustered by the keg out on the deck. My son's electric guitar wailed and a graduate student's electric bass thumped, as colleagues and student writers milled outside and in, throughout the house.

By that spring of 1989, Jeannine was already a close friend. A gifted artist, she had taken poetry workshops from the time I began teaching at the University of Texas at San Antonio in 1982, and within a few years had moved from being a special-student-as-peer to friend. At the party, she walked through the front door carrying a bundle with such care I thought she was bringing a kitten, a puppy, or a baby. She moved right to me, and unwrapped a handwoven blanket, revealing four cloth dolls.

I was speechless. They were dolls unlike anything I had ever seen. She had bought them in Lima, she said, while visiting her daughter who is married to a Peruvian novelist. Hand-sewn by local artists, the dolls are facsimiles of figures integral to the Chancay people's burial practices. The dolls represented family and friends of the deceased and were placed alongside the corpse in the grave. Contemporary Peruvian artisans use ancient fabrics recovered from graves to recreate the dolls. Later, Jeannine told me many in Peru feel the artisans are encouraging the plunder of ancient sites. Others apparently argue that the grave robbing would occur anyway and the reconstructed dolls help resurrect and represent early Peruvian history.

But when Jeannine presented me with the four figures, I knew none of this. I stared at the dolls' stark faces, their geometric features, their bird-like hands, and the gauze fabric of their veils and skirts. It seemed I was in the presence of something inexplicably powerful. I was so drawn to the dolls I could barely continue hosting the party. Memories and associations streamed through my mind, and I wanted to follow them.

Just as the dolls for the dead had been resurrected—or their fabrics retrieved—from the grave, so had an unsatisfied childhood desire been yanked from the stony depths of memory. As a little girl, I had loved dolls. I wanted dolls for Christmas. I was no tomboy; I loved the faces of dolls, their clothes, their sleek hair, arms and legs. I particularly lusted, around the time I was six, for "Story Book Dolls." Named after female characters in fairy tales (or other stories), the dolls were six or seven inches high, with satiny and lacy dresses, their skirts so wide they made a full circle around them. But although my friends collected the dolls and hung them in bright rows across their pastel bedroom walls, my limited allowance seemed unable to stretch far enough to buy one. The only "Story Book Doll" I could save up for was a little girl doll, whose short skirt could not spread out around her. She was not even a character from a recognizable story. I am not sure why I never received one of these beautiful dolls for Christmas; I suspect I was afraid to ask.

If not for Jeannine and her gift, I would never have spent the next several months learning why those little dolls carried so much significance for me. And I would not have realized that dolls—which can seem so trivial, frivolous—are not trivial at all. Not only are they figures children can identify with, or aspire to, but dolls are also similar to religious icons, the statues and retablos of saints: the very stuff of art. Hung on a wall, the way my friends displayed them, they looked almost like little shrines, like images of saints in their niches along a cathedral wall. The Story Book Dolls also taught children something of Grimm's fairy tales, not unlike the way the stained glass windows of the Gothic cathedrals taught preliterate Northern European worshipers stories from the Bible.

But how to get this range of associations into one poem? "For Want of Dolls" went through more revisions than almost any poem I have ever tried to write. The first draft I include is an early one, still a shapeless ramble. Bubbling to the surface was a need to express my childhood sense of dislocation in Arizona, how much I missed my early roots in New Jersey, with its luxuriant deciduous trees and lush summer flowers. This draft is written in third person, a way of distancing myself from the poem. It was a painful subject, I was discovering, and a cavernous one for me. Dolls had been a way of recovering some of the flowery beauty of my grandparents' house and garden, and also, perhaps—in that I could hold a doll, fuss over her, talk to her—of their lavish affection. I missed my grandparents painfully, and saw them only once year. Arizona in the late forties and fifties I felt to be an abandoned wasteland. I could not have put it like that then, but that was how I felt: abandoned, in a wasteland. I talked "funny," my parents talked "funny" (especially my English mother, who taught me to spell all wrong: two ll's for "travelling," "colour" for "color"). No one else seemed to have books in her house, or pictures of anyone but relatives on her walls. I made friends, but it took at least ten years before I began to appreciate the desert's subtle beauty. The poem's subject ran so deep, was so painful and complex for me, I had a hard time containing and shaping it.

As a writer, I need support. Even now, Jeannine is the reader who first responds to my drafts, usually read out loud over the phone. But "For Want of Dolls" received more help from more people than any poem I have ever published. While I visited the Gilberts at their Sea Ranch house in July, Sandra pointed out places that were not clear. The poem needed radical cutting, she said. She was right. I cut, drastically, and tinkered and fussed. I took the poem to poetry groups. When Pat Mora and I spent a leisurely October morning together, she suggested more cutting and clarifying. I continually retitled the poem. It started out as "The Woman Who Wanted Dolls," changed to "On Wanting Dolls," to "On Collecting Dolls, Stories to Live With," to "Dolls of the Dead," and finally ended up with the more suggestive "For Want of Dolls." By the time I was close to finishing the poem, practically every one of my friends had helped. And each response helped me better understand what I was trying to do.

It was my son, by that time fifteen, who insisted late one night when I was in despair over ever completing the poem, that I change the order of the sections. The part about France was the most moving, he said, and the poem needed to start where the poem had actually begun: with the offering of the dolls. Much earlier, in one series of drafts, I had started the poem that way, but for some reason had abandoned that order. No wonder David is now a gifted composer, performer, and producer of music; he was right. With this rearrangement of sections, the poem was close. Most of the rewriting from that point involved weaving images, words and sounds, within the poem, so it reads coherently, has its own music, so the separate sections resonate back and forth. For instance, the dolls' mouths are described in the first section as "ovals," and the faces of the dolls' babies are "pale." In the poem's last line, the faces of Mary and the Christ Child in Chartres' north window are described as "pale, oval faces." The poem is filled with *l* sounds, soft *e* sounds, and the *d*s of "dolls," and "dead," and "doves." Arranging the poem in triplets helped to tighten and compress the poem, to shape it and provide a more unifying—if still loosely woven—structure.

A few months after I followed my son's suggestion, *The American Scholar* accepted the poem, and a few months after that, the editor informed me it had won the Mary Elinore Smith Prize for 1991. I feel as though, Oscar-style, I want to name all the people here who helped with the poem: Jeannine Keenan, Sandra Gilbert, Pat Mora, Walt McDonald, Sherry McKinney, Melissa Shepherd, Cyra Dumitru, Barbara Stanush, Veda Smith, Vera Banner, Sharon Godbey, Laurence Barker, David Barker, and Mark Allen. I know I am leaving someone out.

I had never asked so readily for so much help with a poem before. I was—and still am—amazed so many were willing to make suggestions for this poem. And as the revision process continued, I began to realize the poem is as much about offering, about giving, as it is about the artifacts of dolls, or religious iconography, or art. It was Jeannine's gift—and the way she gave it, tenderly unwrapping the blanket, bending over the dolls, and extending her arms with them—that brought something alive in me again.

The dolls themselves I hung (carefully, so as not to tear their fragile fabric) on the wall above my desk, their geometric faces before me as I worked. Later, I devised writing assignments based on my own experiences writing the poem. Think of an old toy you cherished, or one you always wanted but never received, I have said, and describe it. Write about what you now realize it represented to you as a child. For toys are metaphoric, as is art. And so are the gifts from friends.

❖ WAY OF WHITENESS ❖

The Poem

WAY OF WHITENESS

> ...until the whole field is a
> white desire, empty, a single stem,
> a cluster, flower by flower,
> a pious wish to whiteness gone over. . . .
> —W.C. Williams

All month the moths hovered,
bits and slaps of white pricking
the green mist: yarrow
at Fountains Abbey, dotted blossoms
clustered among leaves and branches, the white
rumps of lazing goats on the hills,
two white horses, muscles
grazing moorland above the Haworth parsonage.

This summer I have been tracking whiteness.
Clusters like doilies, caps, crowns,
but away from our own country
we aren't sure of the names.

You said elderberry, it could have been Queen Anne's Lace.
And on the train the row after row of windows,
one after the other, rhythm of lines
of trees bordering fields, furrows.
The colors friends wore changed daily,
jackets of jade and pink, yellow, green, brilliant
as the crème de menthe at one time
I had thought a fancy drink.

Until this trip I had never had time to walk
behind Chartres, to stop and face the row
of white blooming trees, hawthorns, I finally decided,
masses of white clustering sweet flowers.
Tree after tree, each one almost
as tall as the cathedral.

In Strasbourg on the river blackening one night
someone spotted a swan and suddenly
there were dozens gathered in a cove
of the river, a progression of white neck after
white sliding into the dark.
Miracle of sweet milk in coffee.
Dissolving.
Until, finally, at Canterbury, there was only this: white
clouds sweeping behind a spire, the spire
easing into the white
sky filling vision.

And this was even before the music
filled the interior spaces
of the choir at Evensong.

About the Writing

I n a few hours I am going to the funeral of the one of the friends I traveled with the summer I wrote the poem. Katy Peachy never talked unless she had something to say, which invariably would be pithy and wryly observant. She and her husband Howard were about twenty years older than I, but somehow I never thought Katy would actually die. She was too gritty, too sensible, and, whereas I have often thought of other older friends (even people not much older than I) with concern about infirmities and longevity, I never had a qualm about Katy, and just assumed that she would live well into her nineties. She died three days ago, at eighty-one, while napping.

Katy was not, however, the focus or even the impetus for the poem. But she and Howard were among those whose company stimulated and sustained me on the group tours my former husband organized during the 1990's after he left teaching and choral directing.

Most of all, I looked forward to the trips when David Dooley, a paralegal and fellow poet, would be along. We showed each other drafts we scribbled on the long train trip between Paris and Madrid. We took long walks after dinner in Ravenna while the heavy drinkers grew rowdy. We stuck together in the Prado, trusting that neither would break the other's concentrated immersion in a painting. We knew neither one of us would leave before the other was ready, or take too long over any single canvas. Quietly, we could pay attention to a painting as it revealed its patterns and layers. We laughed together, shared a similar sense of humor. And the fact that David was gay helped too; we could openly ogle male bodies on and off canvases.

I realize now that during those years I was unconsciously preparing to leave my bibulous husband, and David provided a steady yet stimulating companion during lonely times. In retrospect, I realize he even helped me see what might be possible in a future mate—my companion now shares several of David's most congenial qualities.

"Way of Whiteness" was written after a walk I took with David in Canterbury. I had been there before, so skipped the morning group tour, caught up on sleep, and after lunch agreed with David to (re)visit the Cathedral. He had just taken the tour and, with a particularly endearing gleam in his eye, assumed the role of guide, saying: "Follow me." He led us through streets that narrowed and narrowed; I did not recognize them.

But suddenly, we burst through the gates, and there it was: the cathedral. There was no one else present; perhaps an afternoon service had begun. I bent my neck further, looked up, and up. The clouds were moving. The cathedral spires were moving. The earth was revolving, the universe, all of us, at the same slow pace, we were all in circular motion, we were all one. I do not know how long it was by the clock before I turned to look at David. When I did, everything had changed, shifted. David didn't say a word, just smiled. We strolled back to the hotel in a clear light, steps brisk. My husband was napping. I wrote the poem, almost whole, almost as it appears here.

When Katy Peachy came to a signing at which I read the title poem from my newest collection, "Way of Whiteness," she commented afterward: "Thank goodness you didn't reveal our names." I want to name her here. And David Dooley.

❖ TO THE DOGS, IN SOFIA ❖

Abandoned Poem

THE DOGS OF SOFIA

A woman's head from a basement window,
a restaurant, behind her a table of olives, peppers,
onions and oil, but she is feeding the dog
with teats sweeping the leaves on the sidewalk,
its tail wagging, not leaving.

*

Grizzled, head lowered, eyes forward,
the brown dog on San Stefano is barking, insistent,
repeated, unstopping. A car is trying
to park on the spot of the sidewalk where
the dog will not give ground.

*

Little white-eared black dog curled in a crumpled
pile of leaves and plastic bags by the curb
across from the front door to 28 Marin Drinov
where one of the tenants when she leaves in the morning
hands it a heel of bread. Even a sausage.
Odd hours the dog watches, an eye closing,
an eye opening.

*

In Doctor's Garden the leaves on the paths
are of no use to anyone. A rotweiler pup tugs
at an old tire. Bites it, snaps, snarls, backs off, leaps,
and scoots it through the leaves,
turns it upright, and rolls.

October 2000

Another Abandoned Poem

STRAYS

Thousands. Unattached
to leashes, arms, or human

voices. Although the bitch
with swollen teats swaying

to the sidewalk feeds at noon
from a hand reaching

through a basement window
and the black dog who curls

at night in the hole
between a building's stones

waits daily for the slight
woman who swings

the door and hands the dog
half a loaf, a cube of beef.

Not all the dogs are lost.
Not all of us are found.

(Sofia)

June 2001

About the Writing

I gave up trying to write a poem about the dogs in Sofia. I am sure a better writer than I am could have written a magical poem about Bulgarian dogs, but I am not yet that poet. After tinkering with dozens of prosy, fragmented, and unsatisfactory drafts, I finally realized that I wanted to expand, to explore and explain, without fiddling with form, without being stopped by line breaks. I turned what I had hoped would be a poem into an essay, which follows this one.

As "To the Dogs, in Sofia" makes obvious, I found much about living in Sofia bewildering. Before arriving in Bulgaria to begin our Fulbright lectureships, my companion and I had been coached to expect confusing contradictions. Nodding the head up and down in Bulgaria means no; turning the head from side to side means yes. But contradictions extend to matters of street survival as well. Sidewalks are often used as car parks, so that pedestrians must negotiate around cars to walk in the street for a half block, or a block or two, before returning to the relative safety of the sidewalk. Even when a stretch of sidewalk appears invitingly bare of parked vehicles, it can still contain hazards, and not only dog droppings. Sidewalk stones are uneven, tilted, wobbly, and are frequently missing entirely. Once we looked down through a dark gap in the sidewalk, but could not see to the bottom. No wonder former Fulbrighters had injured ankles. We were lucky; we broke only shoes and toenails.

For the first couple of months we lived and taught in Sofia, I was still struggling to read the Cyrillic alphabet, and had to spell out slowly the names on street signs before I knew where I was headed. Since when I walked (and we walked everywhere, to teach, to shop for groceries, to stand in line at the police station for ID cards), I was constantly on guard against errant sidewalk stones, dogs, dog leavings, and, while walking in the street, against speeding Mafiosi's Mercedes, I found it difficult to struggle simultaneously with street signs and unfamiliar landmarks.

Of course, inside our apartment, I could relax. But even there, I felt disconnected. Our e-mail system functioned sporadically. The phone worked when the other party was not using it but had no long-distance capability. I missed my son, I missed friends, I missed using the English language. I missed books, the mail. I missed being able to speak in nuances, with humor, in familiar colloquialisms. I missed people with whom I had a shared history, a degree of intimacy. I enjoyed my colleagues, my students, was making friends, had found the markets, learned the most necessary streets, the names of vegetables, but I did not belong. And even though the support of my companion did wonders, I often felt as peripheral and mute as the unowned canines who roamed the streets.

In time, I became deeply fond of friends we made in Sofia, especially of fellow writers. And I came to feel a great respect for the Bulgarian people. They have had as hard a time as the dogs, or harder, their mountains and valleys ruled by the Turks for five hundred years, then by the Germans, and then by the Soviets. Now, finally free of external tyrannies, the country is finding the shift to capitalism painful. Corruption is rampant, unemployment is epidemic, and abortions are more numerous than births. Bulgarians are undergoing an identity crisis: who are they, free finally of the Ottoman and Soviet yokes? Bulgarian young people want to come to the United States, and do. Over a million people have left the country—for North America and Northern Europe—in less than a decade. And yet the Bulgarian people I came to know were filled with good humor, energy, patience, and endurance.

In contrast, I seemed to lack all these qualities as I tried to adjust. At times I wondered why I was there. I developed deep empathy toward anyone who has to relocate, leaving a language and loved ones behind. No stranger to moving (I attended over a dozen schools in twelve years), I had still never spent more than a month in a country where my native language worked with only a select few. And with no friends around for long phone talks, few books in English available for good reads, no cosy house to putter in, I had to find out who I was without the people and places—the intersections, interstices, the spaces (both psychological and physiological)—that had previously defined me. (I am embarrassed to admit that I actually found printing out my curriculum vitae comforting—there in black and white was at least something of who I was.) But as the essay suggests, I slowly came to feel less lost, until one day, in the Minimart downstairs, I found myself shaking my head from side to side to mean yes, without giving the gesture a second thought. The family who owned the little grocery were my neighbors. I lived upstairs. We were connected. I was connected. In that one gesture, that had suddenly become part of the way my body moved in space, in relation to others, I had become, paradoxically, more myself, and at the same time, more Bulgarian.

I am still not sure why I could not have developed this subject as a poem. The first piece I include here, written while in Sofia, in October, shows my joining several journal entries together, hoping these descriptions of various dogs could be worked into a poem. But I was stuck—did not know where to take the piece next. The second abandoned piece I include, written at home in San Antonio, a few days before I began writing the essay, shows my making the connection between the dogs and myself, but is still undeveloped. Perhaps in this instance I needed the essay form in order to say something straight out (not "slant," to use Dickinson's word), without focusing on compactness, on sound and line. But the essay is as built around metaphor as any poem. I guess, like the homeless dogs, I needed a certain amount of freedom to wander around, without a leash or line breaks, to find the door step where I would eventually curl up and write what I had to say. Strange: this was one of the first times it was prose that allowed me to lose myself enough that the writing could be found.

TO THE DOGS, IN SOFIA

For most of my life I have lived with dogs. Albums in my family are packed with snapshots of English cockers, a German shepherd, border collies, Irish setters, a Great Dane, and numerous mutts. On her walls my mother has framed as many photos of her dogs as of her grandchildren. But I was not prepared for the dogs of Sofia.

Neither was I prepared for the blurring of what had always seemed to me firm categories: sidewalks are, by definition, for walking, or at least, had been, in my clear-cut American mental glossary. And a dog outside, unattached by leash or voice to an owner, was lost.

So in Sofia, where I lived and taught during the fall of 2000, and where large numbers of unowned dogs freely roam the sidewalks, I was confused. In the United States, if I saw a dog that appeared homeless, I would be gripped by concern: someone needed to rescue that dog. Could I take it home? Should I take it to a vet? The shelter? If no one claimed it, it would be "put to sleep," or "put down." And of course, I always decided that I had more to care for in my life than I had already bargained for, and that I could not bring home a stray.

There are thousands of dogs wandering about in Sofia, in no apparent relation to any human. Oh, there are plenty of well-groomed dogs on leashes, tugging at them in good European or American urban fashion, straining to sniff the next lamp post, or obediently trotting at heel. As anyone will tell you, Bulgarians love their dogs. But as one walks the streets of Sofia, one brushes past almost as much canine fur as clothed human flesh. And one is constantly navigating not only the uneven stones of Sofia's sidewalks but also the plentiful offerings of canine droppings in various stages of freshness.

The streets of central Sofia are also lined with tall and luxuriantly leafing trees, and there is much to enjoy, the delights of vegetable stands, the intricacies of nineteenth-century architecture, and the spaciousness of parks; the presence of dogginess is not the only focus of one's vision while walking in the Bulgarian capital. But trees, impressive gray stone buildings, and good produce and parks are all characteristic of most major European cities. In the largest city of Bulgaria, I did not expect to vie for sidewalk space with a dozen dogs within one short block.

And cars. I did not expect walking ability to be impeded by the presence of cars parked on the sidewalk. Sidewalks are for people, I can imagine pre-school children chanting, but not in Sofia. They might be, for awhile, but they are also unofficial car parks in this city, and often one has to walk around an entire block of cars lined up, front grills abutting the stones of a building, back grills poking out into the street. Once I watched a dog barking nonstop at a car trying to park on the sidewalk where the dog was standing. The dog kept barking, ferociously. For several minutes it was a stand-off. Finally the car drove off, at which point the dog curled up on its successfully defended turf. I continued walking in the middle of the street, on the lookout for unparked cars.

I think it was this incident that caused me to realize unowned dogs in Sofia are not necessarily lost. This dog, brown, and spotted, by the way, had claimed this bit of sidewalk as his. I turned around after a few feet to watch again. He was curled up against the building wall sleeping. This was his place.

Gradually, as I established a daily walking itinerary, I found that, whereas at first I had noticed dogs only as ubiquitous examples of the canine species, I was beginning to notice and even anticipate the various and unique canine characters I would encounter. I looked forward to seeing the short-eared light brown bitch with teats dragging to the sidewalk as she poked her head into a basement restaurant window. On that sill, in almost fairy-tale fashion, would be cooling fresh loaves of bread, piles of cleaned fish. I never saw her reach in and grab. But every day I slowed my pace to watch as a woman who worked there reached out handfuls of cooked meat, all the while murmuring the kinds of endearments one utters to a favorite pet. I passed this spot on the corner of Vasil Aprilov and Oborishte at least twice a day, and that bitch was always right there, either gulping down handouts or trotting nearby. I never saw her pups, though, and wondered what had happened to them.

But once I came across some friends who were stopped near my apartment, staring at a small cream-colored puppy. They were thinking about adopting it, they said, and were watching it as intently as anyone would in trying to chose best of litter from a purebred dam. Ultimately, they decided not to take the puppy home, and I had no way of knowing if it belonged to the bitch I watched being fed on the corner, although it certainly could have.

In Doctor's Garden there was the rottweiler puppy—I would guess about six months old—who often played with an old tire. I passed through on my way to and from the university to see him nosing the tire, biting it, snapping at it, barking, leaping, and, most amazing of all, scooting it with his nose like a boy with a hoop. And there was the white dog that I used to see running up Marin Drinov, the street where we lived, with a whole sausage in its mouth. Someone fed that dog daily. The sausage was longer than its tail, and I never saw where the dog took its meal to swallow in private.

Shortly after we settled into our apartment at 28 Marin Drinov, I began to notice the little black dog with a white patch on his chest that quickly got up to move aside when we left the building's front door. From the kitchen window I could watch him walking around in front of our building and the Minimart next door. He was always there, day in, day out, lying on the sidewalk across the street, facing us, in the street, greeting us when we returned from the university, or shopping, or a concert. I noticed that other people from our building spoke to the black dog, and began to realize that the woman downstairs not only greeted the dog, but always handed him something—a hunk of bread, or meat, which he took in his teeth and carried across the street to devour. I began to understand: this was our building's dog. He had found his pack. We were it. The dog went with the territory, he had chosen 28 Marin Drinov.

Who knows how it had started? Maybe one kind apartment-dweller had begun to feed the black dog. And the dog just settled in. When it turned cold and began to snow, the black dog began spending his time in a small gap in the street-level stones of our building. And then, more and more, I found him curled up on the second-floor doormat outside the apartment of the woman I had seen feed him. She must have let him in. I began to let him in too, whenever he was outside and I was going in, or out. The first time I did, I followed him upstairs, and watched from the landing as he curled up outside her door.

By strict definition, this dog was no longer a stray. He had an address, our building. And, in the last month we lived there, I began to feed the black dog too, deciding not always to save the leftover rice for our next day's dinner, but to leave it out for our communal dog. He was not all that tame, did not wag his tail and stick around for patting, but he certainly knew where to get what he needed. Months now after returning to my home in the States, I would like to e-mail a neighbor and ask if the little black dog is still there, but I think I know the answer.

I am not naïve or unrealistic enough to suggest that the thousands of unowned dogs in Sofia do not present an almost unsolvable problem. But

I do find a connection between the fact that about the time I began feeding the little black dog I also found myself, spontaneously, in our next-door Minimart, shaking my head sideways to mean yes. In a country where nodding the head up and down means no, and where sidewalks are for parking, to be lost—as the old Protestant hymn goes—can sometimes mean to be found.

❖ MY FATHER'S LIVING ROOM ❖

MY FATHER'S LIVING ROOM

Evening papers
crinkled in his lap,
his hands were clean,
nails trimmed short, his signet ring
had no initial.
I read the headlines from the floor,
trying to see inside, squinting to read
the little letters under the thick ones.
He turned the pages slowly.

"Don't bother your father," my mother
whispered. I learned not to. I practiced
quiet, practiced over and over
scales of silences,
learning as long as I didn't
startle him,
I could make my move
when the paper came down.

As we talked I would shiver
from holding in my words,
from not letting them out
too loudly,
from holding my ribs
close as piano keys
so I could sound
his fears.

Handwritten First Draft

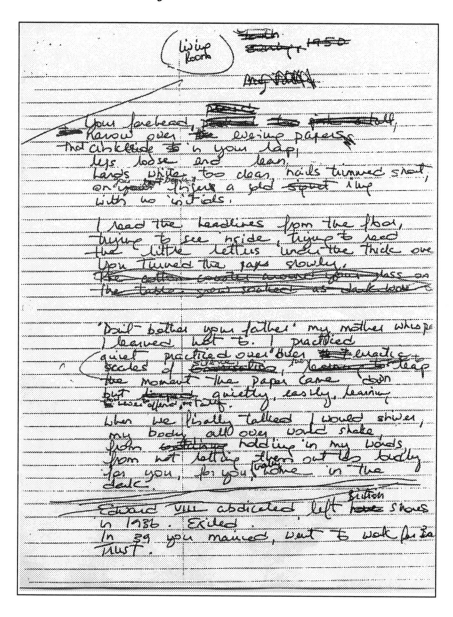

MY FATHER'S LIVING ROOM

Evening papers
crinkled in your lap,
your hands were white, too clean,
nails trimmed short, your ~~gold~~ ring
had no initial.

I read the headlines from the floor,
trying to see inside, trying to read
the little letters under the thick ones.
You turned the pages slowly.

"Don't bother your father," my mother whispered.
I learned not to. I practiced
quiet, practiced over and over
~~scales of~~ silences,
learning I could make my move
when the paper came down
as long as I didn't startle,

When we finally talked I would shiver
from holding in my words,
from not letting them out
too loudly for you

Wendy Barker

About the Writing

When I was six, my father drove me to piano lessons. I remember his soft-spoken warmth in the car beside me, his quiet presence behind me as I fingered simple tunes. But those are the last memories I have of his spending much time with me. After that, I remember his absence—literal, physical, as well as metaphorical, emotional. Evenings, as soon as he came home from the bank, he took off his tie, put on his slippers, and poured the first of a succession of bourbons with ice and soda. I can see his ankles crossed on the footrest of the green and black Barcalounger, his cocktail glass on the wrought-iron table sweating beads of cold water, his umpteenth cigarette curling smoke into the air. Except for his hands and legs, he was hidden from view by the *Tucson Daily Citizen*. When he finished with the newspaper, he flipped through the *Saturday Evening Post,* or *Life*, before turning to one of the Book-of-the Month Club selections piled next to his chair.

I learned very young that I could stay near him in the living room if I did not speak or move. I sat by my father's feet and tried to read the newsprint facing me as he held the pages in his lap. Eventually he might drop the paper and notice me. Some evenings he would be too tired, too distracted, or too worried (or, I realize now, too inebriated) to want much conversation with his eldest daughter. But some times (and oh they were worth waiting for), he would let the folds of the paper rustle to his lap, and ask me a question. I doubt if I ever told him what I was really thinking. I am not sure I knew. I know I grew rigid with fear of uttering something that would cause him, clam-like, to shut closed again. More often than not the dismissal came as a vague "Well now, that's something you should talk to your mother about," or "When you're older you'll understand," and the paper flipped back up into an impenetrable wall, the paternal audience over. The times he scoffed at what I had to say cut so deeply I developed the ability to read him expertly, and learned, I am ashamed to admit, to speak out loud only those notions I thought he might want to hear.

Over twenty years after writing "My Father's Living Room," I am surprised at how much this poem suggests, especially through the image of the piano. Daddy played the piano, often in the mornings before he left for work. As an infant and toddler, already tucked in bed, I drifted to sleep lulled by the cadences of Chopin, Mozart, and Schubert. Sometime in my

MY FATHER'S LIVING ROOM 75

early teens he began taking lessons again, this time branching out into pop. His favorite was "The Poor People of Paris": dee dee DEE dee dee dee dee, dee dee DEE dee dee dee dee, dah dah DAH, dah dah"—every morning. I continued lessons too, although now my mother, admittedly unmusical, drove me. I practiced scales and Bartok when I returned from school, before my father walked in the front door.

He loved music but hated noise. Sundays he would pull LP's from their cardboard jackets and play Wagner's operas, Beethoven's symphonies. I sat cross-legged on the living room carpet, trying not to let my face show the emotions surging inside me. No one else in the family seemed to notice; they faded into other parts of the house. Sometimes my father waved his arms as if conducting, commenting on a particular phrasing. When afterward, I might hum a bit of a passage, his face lit up and he said, "Why, you were really listening!" He seemed amazed that a child of his could appreciate the music he loved.

When the poem first saw print, in 1978, I was racked with conflicting emotions. This was only the third poem I had published, and I was proud. I wanted to show my father. But the poem exposed him, talked of something we had never discussed out loud. I feared he would be furious. He might hate me, never speak to me again. Even so, I mailed him a copy of the magazine in which the poem appeared, *Chomo-Uri.*

Students often talk with me about showing their poems to members of their families. I tell them to be cautious. Early poems, early drafts, are too fragile to bare to people so important. Write what you need to, I urge them, say whatever it is you have to say. Show your work to writer friends and mentors, and ask their reactions, solicit their suggestions. Let your family see a poem only after you are confident you have finished writing it. But I also tell them this story.

Shortly after I mailed off the magazine with my poem, my father called. He seldom initiated the call—it was usually my mother who dialed, talked awhile, and then said, "Daddy would like to talk to you." But this time he called. He had read and reread the poem, he said. He was moved to tears. How could I have understood? Known how he felt during those difficult years in the bank? He had shown the poem to everyone in the office, the vice presidents, the secretaries, and the chairman of the board. He had given a journalist interviewing him a copy of my poem and said, "If you want to know how I felt as a young banker, read my daughter's poem."

I had never before shown my father anything I had created without his finding something to criticize. I do not remember what I said to him that day, but I remember the sunlight in the kitchen, the clean blue of the Sunday afternoon air.

This little poem healed a rift of long-standing between me and my father, and healed a wound within myself. But it was not easy to write. Much of the detail included in the first, handwritten draft had to be cut. The last stanza proved the most difficult (endings have often been hard for me). The second version I include here I had taken to a graduate poetry workshop at the University of California at Davis. The group suggested that the poem ended on too easy an irony:

> When we finally talked I would shiver
> from holding in my words,
> from not letting them out
> too loudly for you
> finally home
> with your children.

I worked and reworked, and when I finally came up with this version, I knew I was close:

> When we talked I would shiver
> from holding in my words,
> from not letting them out
> too loudly,
> from holding my ribs
> close as piano keys,
> so I could hear
> your fears.

I still like the added simile in which "my ribs" are compared to "piano keys," an image that emphasizes the unnaturalness of not making noise—piano keys are designed, after all, to be pushed down, to create sound. In this poem I was learning about developing a good image, letting it expand into a metaphor that works through the poem. But the last two lines were still not right. Although *Chomo-Uri* published the poem with this ending, I was never happy with the sing-song, exact rhyme of "hear" and "fear."

Then in 1990, while revising poems to include in my second collection, *Let the Ice Speak*, I decided to use the word "sound" in the next-to-last line instead of "hear." I liked the ambiguity that "sound" conveyed, so that the poem ended with a paradox: I kept quiet so I could give "sound" to my father's fears, articulate them, give voice to them, and also, find them, try to measure them, plumb their depths.

Writing this poem allowed me to acknowledge an intuitive under-standing of my father that for years I had denied. In the poem I articulat-ed, perhaps for the first time, how fearful I felt my father must have been. I have since learned from my mother that during the fifties a bookkeeper at the bank was embezzling money and altering the books to make it look as though my father was committing the crime. I do not remember the details, only that, although ultimately the thief was fired and my father pro-moted, for a period of several years my father was terrified. I also know now that some of the bank's clients were Mafiosi and frequently attempt-ed to make my father deals they hoped he would not refuse, although he always did. My mother kept on using her run-down washing machine and refrigerator, even though brand-new ones were occasionally delivered to our door. My father insisted they all be sent back, and he wrote polite notes to his would-be benefactors. All this on a small pay check and what were then "banker's hours," which meant leaving home about 6:30 in the morning and sometimes arriving back as late as 9:00 or 10:00 at night. He worked Saturdays.

One of the only childhood memories my father ever shared with me was of his worst nightmare. A gigantic red, white, and blue waffle iron chased him, he said, and he was helpless to resist its determination to brand him all over his body. I have wondered if perhaps he kept such a distance between himself and his children out of fear that he might "brand" us. I suspect he may have felt "branded," or stamped, or molded by his own domineering father who was overflowing with Yankee confidence and determination. But I will never know. How difficult to try to elicit the story of a man who never talked about himself, who remained as closed up tight as a newspaper rolled in a rubber band and hurled out of reach, turning yellow and brittle, under the porch.

❖ OATMEAL AND MORNING SILENCE ❖

OATMEAL AND MORNING SILENCE

(for my mother)

Maybe it was the one meal
you didn't mind.
At least the house
was silent,

only the sounds of your spoon
in the oatmeal pan,
the clink
of a plate for the toast.

It would have been six
in the morning some years,
seventh and eighth grades
were double sessions,

the bus left at six-thirty,
often before the light.
You knew I could swallow
oatmeal, maybe a soft-

boiled egg, quiet food
with none of the tension
of the ground beef and mashed
potatoes at dinner

when we argued and hissed,
dropped our invectives
like forks on a tile floor,
and made the littlest sister

pick everything up.
Breakfast was liquid
as a pond, alone
with you in the white kitchen,

the mulberry trees outside
still part of the darkness
while I tried to eat
enough cereal

so I wouldn't ache
for my bologna sandwich
by eleven, in Mr. Stutts'
social studies class, memorizing

the exports of Argentina.
You'd already eaten.
Or had you? You didn't talk,
kept our silence on the stove

like a kettle
steadily steaming
before the sun burst through,
my sisters woke,

the day came
to a rolling boil.

Draft

```
OATMEAL AND MORNING SILENCE


Maybe it was the only meal
you didn't mind making.
At least the house
was silent.

We must have made four
different shifts at breakfast--
for you and mine must was
have been the earliest.

I remember the stillness,
only the sounds of your spoon
in the oatmeal pan, the clink
of one plate for the toast.

It I don't know what time it was,
would have been six in the morning
some years, seventh and eighth
grades were double sessions,

the bus left at six-thirty,
often before the light.
You knew I could swallow
oatmeal, maybe a soft-

boiled egg, the breakfast
was always waiting, calm,
quiet food with none
of the tension

of the ground beef and mashed
potatoes at dinner
when we argued and hissed,
dropped our invectives

like silverware on a tile floor,
and made the other sister
pick everything up.
I spilled my milk often.

But breakfast was warm
and liquid like a pond white
alone with you in the kitchen, light,
the mulberry trees still wrapped

in darkness while I tried
slowly to swallow
enough cereal
so I wouldn't ache

for my bologna sandwich
by eleven, in Mr. Stutts'
```

1

```
social studies class, memorizing
the exports of Argentina.

You'd already eaten. Or had you?,
You didn't talk, ~~held quiet~~ our silence
on the stove          kept
like a kettle

calmly, steadily steaming
before the sun
burst through, my sisters woke,
the day came
to a full rolling boil.
```

2

About the Writing

Morning silence is not a luxury, as far as I am concerned; it is a necessity. With enough morning quiet, calm—lack of hurry, and I will perform as an effective and efficient member of society for the rest of the day. I have been told I need to fight this instinct, which is sheer laziness, and discipline myself to bounce out of bed and leap into the world's fray, but one of the few things I know for certain is that this body does not function if I cannot wake at my own slow pace.

During my growing-up years, the nightmares I dreamed while sleeping were pallid compared to the nightmare of waking early for school. It did not help that I hated school, which seemed primarily a tedious, exhausting, and painful interruption to my own reading. And since I had so little time to read on my own, I read at night, after finishing my homework. All day I looked forward to the time when, dishes and homework done, I could read, propped on my pillows until my mother's third or fourth light's-out warning. After that I often continued reading, sometimes for hours, under the sheets with a flashlight. No wonder I had a hard time waking up for school the next day.

But I never thought about my mother's role in the morning until it was my turn to wake my own son for school. It proved to be a task so painful I could hardly tackle it. First, I could barely function before nine myself. Secondly, I empathized far too much with my son's sleepiness, unable to separate his reluctance to wake from my memory of my own childhood difficulties.

At some point during my son's grade-school years, I asked my husband if he would be willing to make our son's breakfast. And somewhere around the time our boy was ten, or eleven, maybe a little older, he began making his breakfast himself. A lonely start to a long day.

I do not remember actually writing this poem. My notes show it was drafted in the winter of 1985, when we had just moved into the house we had been planning to build for three years, and which proved to be a mixed blessing. A small architectural gem, it sat on six acres of native grasses, live oaks, persimmons, and buckeyes. But my husband's and my dream was our son's nightmare: he was stuck in a kind of limbo, neither in town, nor suburb, nor real country, in a small-roomed echo-chamber of a house with two distracted parents and no neighborhood kids. I think my awareness of our son's loneliness in our dream house was too painful for me to face head-on. What I could do was remember my own difficult mornings as a girl.

I was also, as the poem makes clear, empathizing with my mother. Without missing a day, fully dressed, she woke me every morning and cooked a good breakfast. That quiet time between us, before anyone else in the family waked (although, now I think about it, it is possible that my father might have already left for work), also must have reminded me of my first three years, before my sisters were born, when I had my mother all to myself. Those school mornings of mine were an odd combination of good and bad dream. They were nightmarish because I had not had enough rest and dreaded the coming day of facts, figures, queries, quizzes, and long bus rides with belligerent school patrols who kept us from even humming under our breaths, let alone talking. And they were dreams come true in that it was just Mom and me, alone, in a shimmering primal space, before the intrusion of my noisy, needy sisters.

I am struck now, sixteen years after writing the poem, by the way it evokes not only our kitchen during the years between my tenth and thirteenth years, but also so much of that house in Tucson in the fifties, its daily rhythms. The mulberry trees out front were sticks when we first moved in, but within a few years were tall and sturdy enough for my littlest sister to climb. The oatmeal or soft-boiled egg and toast sat on a white Melmac bowl and plate on the wrought-iron-legged table my mother had constructed one afternoon (that is another story, perhaps a not-yet-written poem). And I can hear my sisters and myself arguing, giggling and shrieking at supper: we three girls ate together before my mother fixed an adult (and quiet) dinner for herself and my father later in the evening, so our evening meals were undisciplined and often raucous. And we did indeed force my littlest sister to "pick everything up." We also teased her slightest mispronunciation, generally harassing her daily. The poem causes me vividly to see her light brown shiny bangs, her brown eyes, and pert, freckled nose. The poem also brings back the crowded classrooms and halls of Roskruge Junior High, at that time Tucson's only junior high school. The day often did boil during the afternoon in Arizona, although in the winter a harsh wind could make walking to the bus so chilling my fingers around my notebook and books would go numb. No wonder those mornings were "warm and liquid," almost prenatal in their sense of sanctuary.

I think the poem's rhythms help to create this mood of remembered peace and safety. There is a hush about the poem's beginning stanzas, which evoke a feeling of stillness, "liquid / as a pond." The only sounds are the sounds of the spoon, and the plate, comforting sounds, of a child being fed by a mother who, even though she may not be an enthusiastic cook, may not "mind" this meal. The poem's first typed draft, which is included here, had already found its basic form in quatrains. Even most of the line breaks are there. The main changes made in revisions were prunings, and tightening and rearrangement of lines. A few arithmetic figurings for numbers of lines and stanzaic possibilities are marked in pencil in this first draft too, but the quatrains stayed. They help to create a calm but steady pace, the sense of space between stanzas neither hurrying the poem along nor slowing it too much. Making the poem all one stanza, for instance, would sacrifice a necessary pause between stanzas two and three, would lose the sense of each stanza as a kind of mini-memory in itself. Since the poem is narrative, couplets or triplets would slow down the lines too much for a sense of continuity, but since the poem is also contemplative, the quatrains seem just right. A minor problem was what to do with the final stanza, which at first was six lines. Separating "the day came / to a rolling boil" to a final couplet was an easy solution. With the final quatrain reduced to two lines, the poem ends abruptly, so we feel the urgency of the coming day's unstoppable pace. And somehow, separating this last couplet places even more stress on the need for quiet time between mother and daughter, on the calm before the storm, which always arrived, and which assumed many forms, both inside and outside the house.

But I regret that I did not realize in 1985 how much this poem sprang from my own longing to provide a calm and steady morning base for my son, about the maternal pain of not being able always to give what is needed. I am glad though, that on weekends we were able to relish unhurried breakfasts, and that even now, when my son comes to visit, we cook voluminous amounts of scrambled eggs, and, if we are not too sleepy, biscuits from scratch.

❖ BAPTISM ❖

The Poem

BAPTISM

Light dim as the crumbled leather
of old books, and Granny next to me
leaning down with her smell of lime cologne,
finger moving across the small black shapes.
She pointed to the clusters in their tidy lines,
barely stopping under each one, as the minister
kept on talking. My baby sister slept
as he held her, no one else
seemed to breathe.
            But Granny's finger led
my eyes on and on, back and forth, down the page,
and then I saw: she reached *the* at the same time
the minister said *the*, and it happened again,
two lines down, and there were *the*'s everywhere
on those pages—"even unto *the* end of *the* world,"
her finger moved as he said the words
out loud, "*the* kingdom, and *the* power,
and *the* glory," naming.

MY SISTER'S BAPTISM

A light dim as old leather gilt-edged books,
and Granny next to me leaning down
with her smell of lime cologne,
her finger moving across the small black shapes,
~~curved and clipped in tidy lines.~~ Tidy lines,
~~She pointed to the clusters, her finger~~
~~barely stopping by each one,~~ as the minister
kept on talking. My baby sister
slept as he held her, ~~and~~ no one else
~~even~~ seemed to breathe. didn't
But Granny's ~~silent~~ finger never ~~stopped,~~
~~and~~ my eye followed, ~~its tapping,~~ leading my eyes on and on, back & forth
and ~~suddenly~~ I saw: her finger   down the page,
reached the at ~~the same~~ exactly the moment
~~moment~~ the minister said the,
and ~~two lines down~~ it happened again, the,
~~the, there were~~ the's
everywhere on those pages:
"even unto the end of the world,"
her finger ~~flew~~ as he said the words
out loud, "the kingdom, and
the power, and the glory,
and I knew my Granny had given it to me,
even while my new sister Elizabeth slept,
my Granny had shown me the white spaces
that filled the black shapes, had taught
me how to fill the blanks, had given me
the secret to the whole code, that it was all
~~simply~~ a matter of naming.

1st Draft

WBarker

5

M y mother's parents fascinated me. Their rare visits from England were tantalizing glimpses into another world, of finely tuned intricacies of speech and manner. To a young girl growing up first in New Jersey and then in Arizona, they were nothing short of magical. Delicious, subtle, heady foreign smells wafted in their wake—the smoke from my grandfather's pipe, the scent of my granny's cologne. I saw my maternal grandfather only three times: once when I was three, once when I was six, and once again when I was sixteen. Granny I knew a little better; I saw her half a dozen times before she died in 1979.

My parents had fallen in love during my mother's first visit to America in 1937; my mother returned to England, but left permanently for the United States in 1939 to marry my American father. World War II's inception meant that my English grandparents could not be present for their only daughter's wedding. The next time my mother saw her parents was after the birth of her second child, my middle sister, in 1945. My English grandparents arrived in New York on the *Queen Elizabeth*'s first voyage after the war.

I remember, at three, at the close of Granny and Grandfather's visit, watching Grandfather pack for the trip back across the Atlantic on the Queen Mary; the folds of his shirts and socks formed intricate puzzles in his luggage, and he carefully explained the theory behind each tuck and turn. To this day I do a superb job of packing. I had a master teacher.

The visit coincided with my sister's baptism. Although my parents were not regular church-goers, my mother had remained loyal to the Church of England. So whereas I had been baptized in a Presbyterian church, my father's parents' preference, my sister was to be baptized by an Episcopalian minister, the closest my mother could come to an Anglican vicar in Summit, New Jersey. At least the service would be from the *Book of Common Prayer.*

The poem describes one of my most profound early memories. I can smell my granny's citrus scent above and beside me, her 4-7-11 cologne. Not the Chanel No. 5 or Arpège of my four-foot-ten-inch American grandmother, swaddled in furs and sparkling with brooches. Granny was sensible, with the clearest skin I have ever seen, pink-cheeked, and as focused as Grandma was vague. Grandma was cuddly and sweet, a cream-centered chocolate; Granny was determined and directive, a Vick's cough drop. If

Grandma incessantly kvelled, Granny kvetched. Both would have been horrified at their granddaughter's use of Yiddishisms.

Whereas Grandma would come in after we were bathed and pajama'd to kiss us good-night and call us her precious darlings, Granny made sure we not only brushed our teeth thoroughly but knew how to do so for the rest of our lives. Granny had been a governess for several years before advancing her social station in marrying Grandfather, and her child-rearing skills never left her. It was during the visit she made when I was six that I remember the tooth-brushing lessons. "Oh my," she said, "What a big house we have here." She then proceeded to brush every tooth in my narrow oral cavity as if we were, room by room, scrubbing down a capacious estate in the English countryside: we started downstairs, brushing every crevice of the mud room, the butler's pantry, and the kitchen, and then moved upstairs to the drawing room, library, and finally to the bedrooms, even the second parlor maid's sleeping quarters. Our family had just moved into a four-room dusty tract house in post-war Phoenix; Granny's turning my inconsequential mouth into a mansion was as amazing as the fairy godmother's outfitting Cinderella for the ball.

Granny and Grandfather visited us that year after an extended stay in China and Japan, where Grandfather had been overseeing the family import/export firm's offices. After Granny led me through the deliriously evocative rooms inside my no-longer-prosaic mouth, we watched the paper flowers Grandfather had brought us from China unfold their floating petals in the basin. I do not remember ever being put to bed quite so contented, quite so ready for dreaming.

But it was their first visit, when I was three, that began a lifetime passion with language. In Margaret Edson's play *Wit*, professor of seventeenth-century poetry Vivian Bearing recalls the moment she discovered the joy of words: as a little one, reading Beatrix Potter at her father's knee, she struggled to sound out the word "soporific." As her father explained the word's meaning, she discovered that the picture facing the story's text showed Flopsy and Mopsy falling asleep. She was ecstatic to find word and image mirroring each other. I will never forget the moment I saw (and it was a new seeing, a new vision) that the group of black squiggles Granny's finger had recently left was identical to the group of squiggles it had just come to, and when at that exact moment the minister's voice said "the," I felt I had found the key to the universe.

In this poem's first draft, I use the title "My Sister's Baptism." It was only later I realized the poem was even more about my own. It seems now amazingly appropriate that I should come to this love of reading and words, of naming, at a naming ceremony. But it is also paradoxical that while we were all professing, in the name of God, that my sister would be called Elizabeth Clarke Bean, I knew her name was Liza. She had been Liza from the beginning, is Liza to this day. During that one ceremony, I simultaneously gained my first insight into the structure of the rules of language, and my first lesson that such rules can be bent if enough of the right people agree on the degree and direction of the bending. Granny was admitting me into the community of language, and to the often untold secret that it is communal agreements that form our linguistic structures.

Most of all, I learned that day the joy of recognition, the spontaneous "aha" of discovery. I had been well prepared for Granny's initiation: my parents both read to me from the time I could first respond to a playful phrase. My earliest memories are of the rhymes of A.A. Milne's *When We Were Very Young*, the adventures of Babar the elephant, and the exploits of Beatrix Potter's rabbits.

But I am afraid if Granny had known the effect of her moving finger, she would have been aghast. After that first visit until sometime in my late teens, she regularly sent packages from England that unfailingly contained at least half a dozen books for me. I devoured them. School work took a back seat. What was the constricted, compartmentalized, metaphorically barren language of my teachers compared to these novels, with their unique smell of British paper and ink, their fascinating characters, and these richly illustrated books of birds, paintings, and dancers? These seemed more vital than any homework, certainly more interesting than fractions, than predigested biographies of American presidents. Somehow, even as a timid preadolescent, I knew that Granny's finger had pointed the way, that a great glory lies in spontaneously following your own eyes, in the private meaning within the public ritual, in the delight over a single word.

❖ FATHER'S FISH ❖

FATHER'S FISH

I have seen them flop and heave
silver muscle on the boat bottom
and these were not those fish.

Rather they were feathers,
amethysts, sunsets,
clouds swirling and gleaming

in a rectangular blue world
he kept perfect: temperature,
pH, plants, clean gravel, all

perfect. And brilliant. Such brilliant
silences.
          Even the mouths
of the neon tetras, of the knife-narrow

black and white triangular angels
opened only the way a cry
in a dream clutches at silence,

the throat tries, strains
to be heard, aches to reach
the ears that stand

on the other side of the glass
but there is no sound, nothing.
And perhaps the ears would rather

watch, only follow with the eyes
the fishy sliverings, the tailings
and questionings round and round

in the water, and forget what it took
to keep it all going: emptying
the tubes, cleaning the white

gravel, replacing the charcoal,
never overfeeding. It may have been
too much trouble.

There is no longer an aquarium
in that house. Now
on a Northern lake I see him

bent in the boat, hands
trembling as he changes
the lure, prepares

to cast over
the lake's blue ridges,
hoping to reach

the mouths of small bass
as they shimmer
under dark rocks, cut

through dark water,
hoping their mouths will open
eye to eye with his,

yet knowing
that the only way
it will happen

will come in the sharp pull
they both hear,
silent, when the hook holds.

FISH TANK

The only glimmering he allowed
was a watery flicker he had to clean
every week,

How all color was reduced to tht one
glimmering fish tank I will never understand,
but there it was, near the old 78
record player and the albums of Chopin.
Reds, purples, neon greens flashing and swerving
around in the water, tails moving in water
like leaves in wind, like tongues speaking
only a silent language of color
in water so clean the white gravel dazzled.
In all those gray walls
the only color, and yet such silence.
Only the bubbling, the steady ripple
of the filter, the water always being cleaned
and cleaned again, in between the bimonthly
trips to the kitchen he made,
dripping gravel bits and cottony clumps of angel hair
all to be rinsed in the kitchen sink on a Saturday afternoon.

Maybe it was too much trouble keeping
it all going. And

I have seen them flop and heave
silver muscle on the boat bottom
and these were not those fish.

Rather they were feathers,
amythests, clouds
swirling and gleaming

in a rectangular blue world
he kept perfect: temperature,
pH, plants, clean gravel, all

perfect. And silent. Such brilliant
silence.
              Even the mouths
of the neon tetras, of the knife-narrow

black and white triangular angels
opened only the way a cry
in a dream clutches at silence,

the throat tries, strains
to be heard, aches to reach
the ears that stand

on the other side of the glass
but there is no sound, nothing.

                    *

One round eye circling in the pale
water in the toilet, one of them dead
again. If it weren't for the fact

that when they begin to die they float
unsteady, some internal ballast
finally going, wobbling up to the top

where in the end they float
one side up, as if half
of them now denies this watery

life, half of them stares
at the air, the room
outside of the water.

                    *

I remember the sounds of the water,
the rush in the sink, the rustle
of plastic tubes, the strange

gray gravel on the white enamel,
the white cottony wads that he stuffed
in the filter, the regular bubbling

when he got it working right
again. The clarity
of the water, the swirls of turquoise

he painted on the back of the tank
so it looked like deep water
somewhere real, somewhere far

away from Bandstand, homework,
the Barnaby kids in the house behind us
who teased and hollered

even after we'd turned
to go back
inside the fence of our own yard.

                          *

When he took the tank down,
quart by quart of water
back into the kitchen sink,

the few fish left alive
carried on the car seat
in a cardboard carton,

taken back to the fish store,
the dead stayed below the surface
in that house, stayed where they belonged

in drawers of photographs, only
floating up some nights
in dreams, when I'd wake

with voices echoing wild in my eyes.
During the day, the walls of the living room
sat at flat angles to the floor,

the door to the stream, to the blue-silent
silverings closed like an eye
given up to sleep, a face so tired

it could no longer speak
and then I would remember
the guppies, the females .

big and brown and fat-bellied,
dropping their babies
like thistle seeds

on the wind of the still water

2

and I would remember
how the tails fanned

and opened uncurling, sweeping
their silent turnings, their constant,
brilliant revolutions.

*

Now on a Northern lake I see him
in the boat,
old and bent

and fragile-boned, his hand
trembling a little
as he changes the lure.

The boards at the bottom of the boat
weave and rock, their undersides
slick from the black water,

the boat open to the sky
wide-open to the silence
of pine and birch leaf

that glisten around this clean lake
as he prepares to cast
his line over the lake's blue ridges
to reach the mouths

of small bass as they shimmer
over dark rocks, cut
through dark water,

waiting for their mouths to open
eye to eye with his,
hoping their mouths will close hard,

a sharp pull they both hear
when the hook holds.

the mouths opening and closing
as if only in this last encounter
in the silences between

the boards of the boat
weaving and rocking
over black-deep water

the silence between them
says it all

Revision

```
MY FATHER'S FISH

    I have seen them flop and heave
    silver muscle on the boat bottom
    and these were not those fish.

    Rather they were feathers,
    amythests, sunsets,
    clouds swirling and gleaming

    in a rectangular blue world
    he kept perfect: temperature,
    pH, plants, clean gravel, all

    perfect. And silent.  Such brilliant/
    silence.
                Even the mouths
    of the neon tetras, of the knife-narrow

    black and white triangular angels
    opened only the way a cry
    in a dream clutches at silence,

    the throat tries, strains
    to be heard, aches to reach
    the ears that stand

    on the other side of the glass.
    But there is no sound, nothing.
    And perhaps the ears would rather

    watch, only follow with the eyes
    the fishy sliverings, the tailings
    and questionings round and round

    in the water.  And maybe keeping
    it all going was too much trouble
    anyway: emptying the tubes,

    cleaning the white gravel,
    replacing the charcoal in the filter,
    keeping the round bubbles going

    at the just the right pace,
    keeping the algae at bay, and
    never overfeeding.

    There is no longer an aquarium
    in that house.  And now
    on a Northern lake I see him
    in the boat, old and bent

    and fragile-boned, his hand
    trembling a little

                    1
```

He has warned we of the dangers of overfeeding.

little tongues

keys

It may have all been too much trouble.

as he changes the lure,

as he prepares to cast
his line over the lake´s blue ridges,
hoping to reach the mouths

of small bass as they shimmer
over dark rocks, cut
through dark water,

hoping their mouths will open
eye to eye with his,

the mouths opening and closing
as if only in this last encounter
in the silences between

the boards of the boat
weaving and rocking
over black-deep water

the silence between them
says it all

And yet knowing
that the only way
it will happen
comes in the sharp pull
they both hear
when the hook holds,

2

About the Writing

In early September, 1987, my father died. He had been hospitalized for about a month, after surgery for a bowel blockage, from which he never recovered. I missed the first three weeks of the fall semester, and returned to the University of Texas at San Antonio a grieving, weeping shell. What I found on returning, however, waiting for me, was a new community that had actually been there all the time. Many of the graduate students had taken several courses from me before; they ran the poetry workshop by themselves in my absence, and when I returned, they tenderly welcomed me. A number of these students were my age and older, and most had lost at least one parent. During the following fall semester, they became friends, guides through the waters of grief. For the first time, I began bringing in drafts of my poems to my own classes.

That fall I wrote reams about my father, about his life and his dying. He died on a respirator, unable to talk. Well-educated, widely read and highly opinionated, he had never talked about himself to any of us daughters. To me, he had read out loud, had talked about books and music. But about his own life, about anything that had happened or was happening in the family, he was mute. Much of the time he was home, he was simply silent (or trying to be), hidden behind a book or the newspaper.

When my sister and I were little, in the apartment in New Jersey, he had kept tropical fish. According to my mother, when they had friends over for dinner, he would invite the guests into the bedroom where my sister and I were sleeping, saying with a twinkle, "Here is the breeding room," waiting just a moment before pointing to the fish tanks lining the walls not occupied by my cot and my sister's crib. Apparently, the ensuing hilarity would be silenced only by the need to keep us children from waking so the adults could continue their party. I vaguely remember the flickering shapes of the tropical fish whose containers lined my nursery walls. But even though those tanks disappeared for about ten years, my father's love of fish resurfaced during the 1950s. He encouraged me to have a small aquarium of my own in my room, taught me how to feed (not overfeed) the fish, and how to clean the tank. Later still, after my son was born, my husband and I invested in an aquarium, and our dining room was lighted by the shifting jewel tones of tiny fish. We sold the tank and its inhabitants before moving to San Antonio, but after my father died in 1987, I remembered the fish.

Part of what made his death so hard to bear was that, whereas we had been close as young father and young child, as I grew up he became increasingly remote. With the exception of those evenings when he would read lines of poems aloud, or play LP's of Beethoven or Chopin, or the times when he would hand me novels, he was a distant and critical figure. Only after the birth of my son did he develop a tender expansiveness that he displayed mainly with his grandson. He was becoming more kindly than I had known him since my early childhood, and then—he was gone. I had never been able to talk easily and openly with him, and even as he was dying, we could not talk. He could not because he had a fat tube stuck down his esophagus, and I—because I was afraid. Once, as he lay dying, I started to quote a poem by John Masefield he liked, which begins, "I must go down to the seas again / to the lonely sea and the sky," and his swollen body on the white starched hospital bed began heaving and shaking, his head agitated, his hand pawing the air, and I thought he might want me to say the poem he loved most, Frost's "Stopping by Woods on a Snowing Evening," but, like the speaker in T. S. Eliot's "The Wasteland," "my eyes failed," and "I could not / Speak." All around his machine-lined room were glass walls so the nurses could keep constant watch. He might as well have been a fish in a tank.

At the end, we had no words. I could touch him, stroke his arm, stroke his forehead. But with this father who had given me poetry and books, words were denied us. We had to go this last round together speechless.

All my life I had known him as a person whose emotions were seldom expressed, and whose desires were kept on a tight rein, often, I am sure, not even acknowledged. "Don't overdo," was his constant admonition to me, whenever I began laughing, or running. "Don't get too excited." Anything loud, showy, exuberant—he censured. He did not attend church, but the influence of his Scot Presbyterian ancestors bled through in all their gray-grim disapproval of anything that reeked of fun.

No wonder I wrote in the earliest (half-page) draft of this poem, "The only glimmering he allowed / was a watery flicker he had to clean / every week." If joy was not attached to work, to duty, what possible good could it do? Picking the fish tank as an image for my father, I see now, was a good choice, although, as is clear from the three various drafts I include here, it took me a long time of winding around to bring the poem to a conclusion. After I found the poem's central image, its controlling metaphor, I had to find the poem's direction. I had to give it room to expand, which I do in the second draft included here. In this draft I mined memories—

everything I could remember about my father and fish. I began to make the connection between his caring for tropical fish at home and his fishing on Squam Lake in New Hampshire. I was playing with triplets, and by the third draft I include, had cut the poem almost to its final length, leaving only minor prunings left to do. In this draft I separated "And maybe keeping / it all going was too much trouble / anyway" into two segments, so that the much tighter "It may have been / too much trouble" follows "what it took / to keep it all going: emptying / the tubes, cleaning the white / gravel, replacing the charcoal, never overfeeding." The lines create a sense of exhaustion, of the labor of keeping life alive, and of almost giving up, that prepares for the poem's last lines. Finding those lines was difficult; I finally came up with the poem's ending, scrawled in pencil on the last draft included here.

One of the few passions my father acted on, although late in his life, was his love of fishing. Toward the end of his life, he became, in fact, the "grand old man" of the lake, the one from whom younger folks asked advice, asked if Peerface Cove, for instance, was still the best spot. It was lure fishing he loved, small motor boat fishing, the engine no louder than the lap of the water. Loons twenty feet from the prow. He spent hours out on the lake in his last years, and taught my son to fish. It was a quiet activity, like keeping the fish tanks, yet somehow my father's enthusiasm for fishing seemed a healthy development to me. He had moved from a closed world of collecting and controlling fish as tiny, moving *objets d'art* to an open world of currents and creatures often beyond human control. And in the struggle over a taut line, a hook caught and tearing a muscular piscine jaw, he struggled actively with life—and with death.

The way he died, in the ICU, with its multiplicity of instruments, dials, and tubes connected to his exhausted orifices, also reminded me of the fish tanks' tubes, gurgling filters, and thermometers. It was as if he had returned to the tanks, only this time, he himself was caught inside.

I brought all my working drafts to the graduate workshop that fall, and when it came time for the semester to end, realized I did not want to let go of these wise new friends who had helped me weather a difficult season. From that point on I have often brought drafts into my workshops. The students' responses help me, and I find that sharing my own writerly struggles helps them. That December, seven of us agreed to keep meeting once a month with our poems. We continued for years, and even now, join forces whenever a hook seems about to take hold.

❖ NEEDLEPOINT ❖

NEEDLEPOINT

My mother has stitched
a bookmark,
pulled and pushed
a needle, silver-tipped
like my pen,
through canvas,
out, over, under,
prodding the point
into just the right place,
the same way she worked
a needle to lift splinters
from my fingers
when she was my young mother
and I was her young child.

My mother lives in the desert,
she has sewn
while breathing scorched air,
hands dry
from too much heat.
Holding the backing
taut, drawing through
small holes
the soft, curling yarn,
spiraling over and
over the blue
and the green,
she has sewn,
so that I
won't lose
my place.

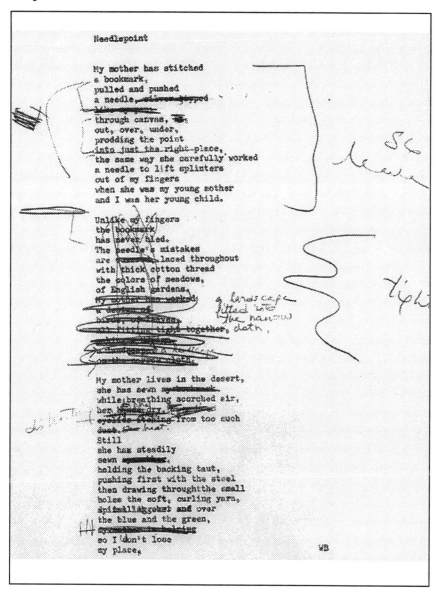

Needlepoint

My mother has stitched
a bookmark,
pulled and pushed
a needle, ~~between~~ ~~slipped~~
~~its~~
through canvas, ~~its~~
out, over, under,
prodding the point
~~into just the right place,~~
the same way she carefully worked
a needle to lift splinters
out of my fingers
when she was my young mother
and I was her young child.

Unlike my fingers
the bookmark
has never bled.
The needle's mistakes
are ~~~~ laced throughout
with thick cotton thread
the colors of meadows,
of English gardens,

My mother lives in the desert,
she has sewn ~~~~
while breathing scorched air,
her ~~~~ dry,
~~eyelids~~ ~~~~ from too much
~~dust,~~ ~~~~ heat.
Still
she has steadily
sewn ~~~~.
holding the backing taut,
pushing first with the steel
then drawing throughthe small
holes the soft, curling yarn,
~~spiralling~~ ~~~~ and over
the blue and the green,
~~~~
so I don't lose
my place,

WB

About the Writing

Only recently have I stopped writing my name in my books. In her collection of essays titled *Ex Libris*, Anne Fadiman humorously describes various readers' attitudes toward the handling of books. Some people refuse to soil their pages with so much as an initial on the flyleaf. I have always told my students, "Write in your books! Argue with the writer! Underline, asterisk, star, check! Refute! Effuse!" My companion finds this advice heretical, sacreligious. Marking any text with even a small dot is a desecration, an act from which he recoils with horror. And during the past few years I must admit I have found it redundant, even a little silly, to inscribe my name in the books that enter my shelves.

As a child I painstakingly wrote my full name in my books: Wendy Wakelyn Bean. (I still love my middle name, have wished I could change my name to "Wendy Wakelyn.") Sometimes the ink leaked in blobs from my Sheaffer's fountain pen. As a teenager, I would add the date I purchased the book, and sometimes I noted the place where I had found it. As a graduate student, my bibliophilic impulses fully unleashed, I indulged in bookplates, often symbolic: a black and flame-colored spiraling shell, a white egret in flight.

But I used all the bookplates, and now most of my new books find their way onto the shelves without my name. I still write with a pencil in hand, and still occasionally make backward check marks (I am left-handed and finally gave up trying to write check marks the "right" way) at points I want to remember, even squiggly lines running down beside a whole paragraph. I no longer write "Ugh," or "Yay," or "What BS!!!" in the margins, but I do sometimes mark little asterisks. Many of my books are filled with yellow stickies blooming from their tops like faded daffodils, but I find the pads of Post-Its® are lasting longer and longer. Gradually, slowly, I seem to be moving away from the camp of those who write in their books.

But nothing will persuade me to relinquish my collection of bookmarks. Long ago I learned how much turning down page corners can damage books; a dog-eared page can tear right off, an unsightly missing triangle. I like my pages unbent, unfolded, even if they are hidden under yellow Post-Its® or cluttered with inked comments. I have bookmarks from Istanbul woven like miniature carpets, bookmarks from Italy cut from leather still smelling like the Mercato Nuovo in Florence, and bookmarks from India carved from sandalwood to look like tiny elephants. I possess embroidered bookmarks trimmed with lace or ribbons that were given to me by students. I have bookmarks from book stores around the country. But the queen of the collection, its Kohinoor diamond, is unique. Thicker than the others, it is backed with white grosgrain ribbon and worked in needlepoint with fine wool. On a white background, a slim green stem spirals and sprouts small green leaves, blue flowers with yellow centers, and red and black lady bugs. My mother made it.

She used to make all our clothes, as well as her own. She was a gifted seamstress, but that is too narrow a definition for my mother's talents. In the 1950s she designed skirts and blouses boldly decorated with colored braid and ribbon. We three sisters all had felt skirts with appliquéd felt designs decorated with sequins. My mother's own clothes were so beautiful she won awards in Tucson and could have sold clothes to all the fashionable ladies in town if my proud father had not forbidden her. And her abilities with needle and thread were not limited to clothes that were finished on her Singer sewing machine.

Among my earliest memories are those of her teaching me to knit and to cross-stitch. I stitched and knitted happily in odd hours for years, always relishing the colors in my hands, the design growing, the precision and flash of a needle. During the 1960s I began working ambitious stitcheries. I was as adept at French knots as I was at herringbone and satin stitches, and the boldness of the stitches grew as my vision for designs deepened. I began to weave and was told by the instructors I was a gifted weaver. Colors and textures ran through my fingers like water, and the thump, thump, of the woof steadied me like a heartbeat. Once, on a weekend at Morro Bay, my former husband and I visited a studio of loom makers. I knew if I were going to continue weaving, I needed to invest in an eight-harness loom. Together we examined the choices of looms offered in the studio, redolent with the clean smells of hand-rubbed wood. "Go ahead," he said. "You need one. We can put it on Mastercard." But I hesitated. I was suddenly overwhelmed with a sense of claustrophobia and walked outside, leaving my husband to chat with the studio's owner.

Listening to the words exchanged between my husband and the loom maker, I had not been picturing skeins of bright threads and intricate designs. I had begun thinking of the book store we had passed down the street. I stayed outside less than two minutes, and came back inside and whispered to my husband that I did not want to spend money on a loom. In a matter of seconds on the sidewalk, I had realized it was time to leave weaving and fabric art. As much as I loved working with thread and wool, fabric art was silent, mute. I needed words, the colors of their sounds, the textures of their patterns. Even obscene words had their own kind of beauty. Syntactical patterns had their forms, like warp threads, their ability to create something whole. Even more than I wanted to collect pale feathery moss and shimmering threads to weave into tapestries, I wanted to create with words. That spring I determined to get on with my life's passion for writing and books. Almost thirty, I resigned from my job teaching ninth-graders in West Berkeley. In June I began graduate work in English.

When my mother gave me the bookmark, I had already received an M.A. in English and was in the midst of earning my Ph.D. I do not know if my mother ever knew what a talisman her gift became. I felt it to be a blessing from my active mother, who seldom sat down quietly in one place, and who, I think, never completely understood the patience it takes to sit for long periods and read, or write. Of course, she sat for hours sewing, but her body was busy. The bookmark said to me, " I am with you as you do your reading, as you work toward this goal so important to you." The bookmark carried my mother's touch.

Around this time I had a dream: that I walked out of a cramped, dimly lighted room filled with women whose necks were bent down over their sewing. I descended a staircase and found myself in a spacious university hallway, with bright, natural light streaming in from floor-to-ceiling windows and open doorways. In my graduate work, in planning to find an academic position, I was in fact leaving my childhood world's definition of "women's work," and was audaciously (and fearfully) striving for a goal that to my mother's and father's generation was not "feminine." I was painfully aware that I was trying to push past an earlier era's commonly held definitions.

The bookmark somehow spoke volumes. My mother often told me how much she loved reading novels, poems, and plays at school in England. If she could have gone on to college, she said, she would have studied literature. Somehow her gift helped mark much more than my place in a single book. It stood for a woven connection between us. The design's green spiral with leaves marking places on the way served as a reminder of the way the bookmark itself could mark each page, one page at a time, helping me keep my pace, so my goal would not seem overwhelming.

My mother's childhood, about which I know so little, was spent in England and Hong Kong in luxury unimaginable to me. I do not know how she managed to bring up three girls on a tight budget in Tucson after having been carried to school in rickshaws pulled by coolies. But she did manage, and through that succession of dreary tract houses in which we lived throughout the fifties, she infused our lives with a bit of dazzle, a soupçon of panache. It was years later I realized she was not only making clothes: she was doing the best she could as a woman of Pat Nixon's generation to make art, to bring something beautiful into drab surroundings. And beauty, D.H. Lawrence (who had known hunger) has said, "is something we humans need more than bread."

❖ BLACK SHEEP, WHITE STARS ❖

BLACK SHEEP, WHITE STARS

He'd appear like a bird
that wanders into a place
on its way between two continents.
Surrounded by houses
that sopped up sparkle like sponges
he'd roll out of a '47 black Cadillac

and wave a bottle of rum
shimmering in the sun like amber.
"Pam, darling," he'd call to my mother,
his voice so raucous
Mrs. Simonitch next door
would move one slat of her Venetian blinds.

His toes pushed from limp huaraches
and he grinned as if he knew
just how much acid
the sight of him
shadow-bearded, yellow under the arms,
produced in my father's stomach.

When he talked
our windows grew arches, opened doors
onto courtyards, lemon trees, parrots,
we could hear the rustling of green feathers,
the chirrings and cawings of orange birds.
Small on the sofa I said

"Let me come live with you,"
something in my lungs knowing
that in a place named Jlayacapan
people might swallow drinks
the colors of bougainvillaea
and move at night

to music that had never heard
of a metronome.
And when Uncle Dick and his friend Pedro
sat me between them
on the Cadillac's dusty front seat
to watch *High Society* at the Frontier Drive In,

I held myself taut and sweaty, dreaming stars
thicker than sugar on oatmeal,
stars farther than heaven,
stars and hibiscus and mangoes
that could cluster around a life
as long as a laugh.

Some years he'd show up
like a bird that wanders into a place
every few years on its way
between the poles of two continents.

He'd roll out of a '47 or '49 black Cadillac
~~dotted with bullet holes as if the car had acne,~~
wave a bottle of scotch ~~or rum,~~
~~the booze still sloshing in the glass~~
that flashed in the sun like ~~crystal~~ amber.

In the middle of all those red brick houses
that sopped up sparkle like dirty sponges.

"Pam darling" he'd holler at my mother, his voice
~~in a voice~~ raucous enough
so raucous that ~~old~~ Mrs. Simonitch next door
would move a slat of ~~the~~ venetion blinds.
~~up a notch with her long nails.~~
We could feel the eye watching.

His ~~man's~~ toes pushed out of limp hueraches
and his eyes grinned as if he knew
just how much acid the sight of him
(shadow-bearded, yellow and wet under his arms)
~~oxford-cloth arms)~~
could produce in my father's stomach.

He'd shudder
~~His voice would shudder~~ my father
from his chair, would shatter the wall ray
of newspaper as he sat on our old ~~gray~~ sofa
telling stories ~~that changed the color~~
~~of the paint on the walls,~~
That turning the room persimmon and tangerine,
~~changing the light to yellow as he~~ chuckled
so loud the small square windows
grew arches, opened French doors onto patios
lined with lemon trees and parrots.

Small on the sofa I said "Let me
come live with you,
something in my lungs knowing
that in a place with a name like Jlayacapan
people might swallow cold drinks red as bougainvilla
and move at night to music that had never heard
of a metronome, the Viennese School, or ~~even~~
Teresa Brewer.

And when Uncle Dick and his friend Pedro
sat me between them on the dusty front seat
~~of the old Cadillac~~
to watch High Society at the Frontier Drive In,
I held myself taut and sweaty
memorizing the jokes and the dancing

that grew like ~~the~~ night *around me*
~~on every side of me,~~
.growing into notions of stars
.sprinkled thicker than sugar on oatmeal,
·stars farther than heaven,
· stars and hibiscus and mangoes
· that ~~might~~ *could* cluster around a life
. as large and ~~as~~ long as a laugh.

Black Sheep and
~~Bright~~ ~~Red~~ Dreams

~~Hard~~

↑

~~Some years.~~ ~~He~~'d show up
like a bird that wanders into a place
every few years on its way
between the poles of two continents.
~~Surrounded by~~
~~In the middle of red~~ brick houses
that sopped up sparkle like dirty sponges
he'd roll out of a '47 or '49 black Cadillac
waving a bottle of scotch

that flashed in the sun like amber.
"Bam darling" he'd holler at my mother / his voice
so. raucous/ Mrs. Simonitch next door
would move/ a slat of her Venetian blinds.

~~We could feel the eye watching.~~
His toes pushed ~~out of~~ limp huaraches
and his eyes grinned as if he knew
just how much acid the sight of him

(shadow-bearded, yellow and wet under his arms)
could produce in my father's stomach.
~~He'd shudder my dad from the newspaper~~ → he'd shatter my father wall
as he sat on our ~~old~~ gray sofa   (of newspaper

telling stories that turned
the paint on the walls persimmon and tangerine,
chuckling so loud
the small square windows
~~grew arches, opened French doors onto patios~~
~~grew arches,~~ opened French doors onto patios
sprouting ~~with~~ lemon trees and parrots.
Small on the sofa I said 'Let me

come live with you,

something in my lungs knowing
that in a place with a name like Jlayacapan
people might swallow cold drinks red as bougainvilla
and move at night to music that had never heard

.of a metronome, the Viennese School, or Teresa Brewer.
And when Uncle Dick and his friend Pedro
sat me between them on the Cadillac's dusty front seat
.to watch High Society at the Frontier Drive In,

.I held myself taut and sweaty
.memorizing the jokes and the dancing
. that swirled like the night around me
.growing into notions of stars

· sprinkled thicker than sugar on oatmeal,
· stars farther than heaven,
~~stars and hibiscu~~

```
BLACK SHEEP, RED STARS


He'd show up
like a bird that wanders into a place
every few years on its way
between the poles of two continents.

Surrounded by brick houses
that sopped up sparkle like sponges
he'd roll out of a '47 black Cadillac
and wave a bottle of rum

that flashed in the sun like amber.
"Pam darling" he'd call to my mother,
his voice so raucous
Mrs. Simonitch next door

would move one slat of her Venetian blinds.
His toes pushed from limp huaraches
and his eyes grinned as if he knew
just how much acid the sight of him

shadow-bearded, yellow under his arms,
produced in my father's stomach.
When he shattered my dad's wall of newspaper
with stories

succulent as apricots or tangerines
our windows grew arches,
opened doors onto courtyards
of lime trees and parrots.

Small on the sofa I said
                        "Let me come live with you,"
something in my lungs knowing
that in a place with a name like Jlayacapan

people might swallow cold drinks red as bougainvilla
and move at night to music that had never heard
of a metronome, the scales in E flat,
or even Teresa Brewer.
```

And when Uncle Dick and his friend Pedro
sat me between them on the Cadillac's dusty front seat
to watch <u>High</u> <u>Society</u> at the Frontier Drive In,
I held myself taut and sweaty

memorizing the jokes and the dances
that swirled like the night all around us,
dreaming stars
thicker than sugar on oatmeal,

stars farther than heaven,
stars and hibiscus and mangoes and laughing,

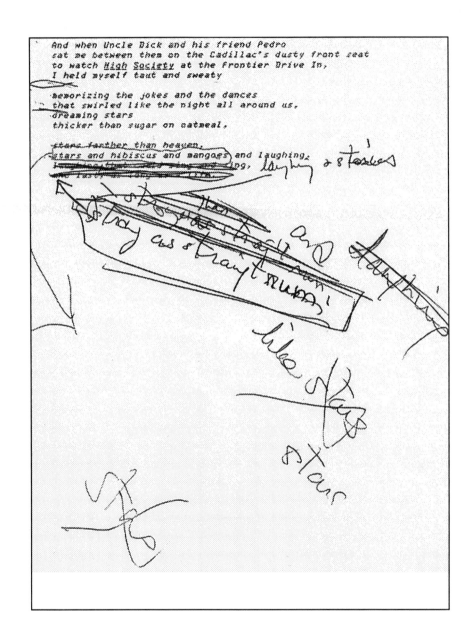

About the Writing

As a child, I often wondered if I had been adopted. No one in my family seemed remotely like me. I did not fantasize, as children sometimes do, that I was a princess stuck in a family of peasants. If anyone resembled royalty in our family, it was not me. Wispy, pale-eyed, pale-haired, gangly, and, according to the general consensus, far "too sensitive," I felt an insubstantial outsider in a family where everyone else stood dark and sturdy. My mother, brown-eyed, dark-haired, stunningly beautiful, and usually in motion, designed and sewed our clothes, built furniture, mowed the unruly Bermuda lawn with a hand mower, and pulled out weeds for hours in one hundred-degree weather. My father worked extended hours even on Saturdays to achieve promotions within a regional bank. Voted Queen of her classroom, my middle sister earned straight-A report cards and filled the wall by her bed with blue ribbons and brass plaques. My youngest sister, brown-eyed like my mother, pretty and graceful, was learning to dance, tap and toe. Me—I had huge feet, asthmatic lungs, and thick-lensed glasses. At recess, I cringed from flying balls: volley-, base-, kickballs alike terrified me. I did not always see them coming, and more than once had been hit in the head. At my athletic best I managed jacks on the sidewalk, with an old golf ball I could keep within close range.

Safe in my own room, I arranged my most precious objects, figurines from my New Jersey grandmother's house, miniature porcelain animals, a thriving philodendron in a ceramic pot, into a series of shrines. At night, I walked out into the back yard, looked up at the Milky Way sweeping its brilliant swath across the clear sky, and wished on a star: "Star bright, star light." My wish was always the same: that some day, someone would love me.

I was of course imagining romantic love. Even at the age of nine I was picturing who "he" might eventually be. But once in a great while, not often enough, a male relative dropped into our lives as if from heaven, and, almost like Cinderella's prince, at least temporarily rescued me.

Uncle Dick was not really my uncle. My mother's favorite cousin, Dick had worked as an artist in Guadalajara since the 1930s. Regarded as the "black sheep" of my mother's family, he had left England to study painting in Paris, where he was befriended by Salvador Dali and Max Ernst, but as Hitler's terror spread, he left France for the United States. He took a train east across Europe, and at some point hopped a freighter, landing eighteen months later in Los Angeles, where he hobnobbed with David Niven and other Hollywood notables, before heading south. He settled in Guadalajara and by the 1940s was a successful portrait painter of political and cultural figures, an occupation that ensured enough income that he could also paint what he wanted.

As a child, I knew none of this. His arrivals were surprises. Suddenly, rumbling in the driveway, would be a dusty, ancient black Cadillac, and, when the engine quieted, his tall, lanky frame would lope up the sidewalk, bringing more energy into the house than it had known since his last visit. I imagine our gray living room suddenly exploding with light and a palette of brilliant color, although he wore yellowed white Oxford cloth shirts, frayed at the collars and sweaty and discolored under the arms. He arrived with a different male friend every time—I barely remember his companions, but about Dick, I remember everything.

I remember one visit when the car he brought was riddled with—the only conclusion my mother could draw was—bullet holes. She had begun, she confided in me, to suspect he was running cars over the border. Or worse. I did not know what "worse" might be, but I did know my father could never wait until he left. My father, always quiet and withdrawn at home, became positively snail-like during Dick's visits. Years later my mother told me it broke her heart—she was continents and oceans removed from everyone else in her family, and Dick was not only closest geographically, but sympathetically, and yet my father did not want Dick in the house. I, on the other hand, wished he would move in.

He had that marvelous British wit which assumes you too are in on the joke, and there is always a joke. Life is a joke. Everything is something to laugh over. People are fascinating and funny, amazing in their variations. And he had that British upper-middle-class intonation, a vocabulary that cascaded delectable words, phrases so precise they opened glass French doors into rooms of precious vases, pianos, and exquisitely, exotically dressed people, phrases opening onto new countries of colors and landscapes of which I had never even dreamed. And best of all, he seemed to like me.

I remember sitting beside him on our gray sofa, drinking in his words, his potent aroma. Of course, he drank. But so did my father and my mother—everyone did in those days. It was what nice grown-up people "of our sort" did. But he did not drink like my silent, withdrawn father. He swung the bottle as he poured, and his stories grew funnier the longer he drank. With me, he was gentle and kind, and always attentive. He listened, and, shy as I was, I found I could talk to him. I do not remember what I said, only that during our conversations I felt alive.

On one of his surprise visits, my parents were out of town, in Phoenix for a convention. We were under the thumb of a grim, leather-skinned baby sitter who refused our requests to watch TV while assaulting us with long passages from Scripture. But to our delight, she was interrupted one afternoon by Uncle Dick and his friend Pedro at the screen door. I imagine we all three screamed and yelped with joy—we had been rescued from the wicked witch. My mother has since told me that when he arrived at the Camelback Inn in Phoenix two days later, surprising her and horrifying my father by breaking into a formal reception line for Arizona bankers ("Pam, darling! Found out where you were from Wendy, thought we'd surprise you!"), he told her that our baby sitter was "a horror" and "darling Wendy especially was in dire need of relief." Somehow he managed to charm the "horror" into allowing him to take me out to dinner and to the drive-in movies, something I am quite sure my father never would have permitted. I do not think Daddy trusted Dick a foot from the front door. Where we had our dinner, I cannot remember, but I will never forget the movie. The sights and sounds of Bing Crosby and Louis Armstrong joking and harmonizing in *High Society* ("Have you heard, it's in the stars, next July-ee we collide with Mars, what a swell party it is. . . .") set free something deep down in me, something that had been almost strangled. Right next to me in the front seat of this battered old Cadillac was someone, actually (unbelievably!) related to me, who was tall, lanky, blonde, and big-nosed like me, who joked and quipped as cleverly as these guys in the movie, who moved as freely as these larger-than-life stars swaying and crooning on the screen. Uncle Dick and Pedro even bought popcorn and soft drinks at the refreshment stand. I was ten, at most, eleven, and I doubt if I had seen more than six movies in my brief suburban life. And even though my parents had taken me and my sisters to the drive-in a couple of times before (*Singin' in the Rain, The African Queen*), they had not allowed us snacks. Simply sitting beside this magical relative evoked nothing short of "True Love." And if intuitively knowing someone and understanding what she needs is love, then he loved me. He recognized how miserable I was— perhaps not just with the baby sitter—and did something about it. And he seemed to enjoy my company as much as I adored his.

After that, I began writing him. In one letter, I secretly asked if I could come live with him. He did not answer me right away, but hastily wrote my mother, explaining that his hilltop hacienda served not only as his home and studio but also as the setting for week-long parties and would not, repeat, not, be a fitting place for "darling Wendy" even to visit, much less come to stay. He need not have worried; my parents would never have allowed me to travel alone to Guadalajara even for a weekend. I do not know when I realized my Uncle Dick was gay, but it was certainly years after the magical evening of *High Society*. I do remember his letter back to me, explaining that he was frantically painting to meet deadlines, that it would be too hard for me to go to school, and that, although he would love my company, it would not be possible for me to come live with him.

I do not remember if I was crushed. What I know is that, without Uncle Dick, I might never have written a word. He showed me a world of people outside the narrowness of our middle-class Tucson subdivision, my often unintelligent and unimaginative teachers, and my parents' dull friends, who were mostly my father's business connections. Dick showed me I could color outside the lines.

I do not know why in 1984 I began remembering Uncle Dick. Maybe it was because living in San Antonio, fairly close to Mexico, revived those old memories, brought them bubbling to the surface. And maybe it was because I was finally doing what I had always wanted, living a life of playing with language, writing, and teaching. The poem came, as the first typed draft shows, almost whole. I find it interesting that even in this early draft, I changed the truth: "Small on the sofa, I said, 'Let me come live with you.'" For the purposes of the poem, I could not go into all the detail of my correspondence with Uncle Dick. But even though I sensed the need for economy, the early draft I include still needed, as so many of my poems do, radical cutting and shaping. By the next draft, I was thinking of dividing the poem into five-line stanzas. In the third version included here, the stanzas have become quatrains. But many of these lines are unwieldy, too long, and the rhythm often falters. Ultimately, the six-line stanzas were a good choice, I think, since they help contain the poem's narrative while also moving it along. Much of the work of the poem became, then, a matter of working on sound. Uncle Dick's waving "a bottle of rum / shimmering in the sun like amber" is much more compact and musical than saying he waved "a bottle of scotch or rum, / the booze still sloshing in the glass / that flashed in the sun like crystal."

For years I was unhappy with the ending. I had become stuck on finding a simile: "as long as a..." As long as a what? Although I am not sure how I would rewrite the ending now, I have wondered at my choosing such an ambiguous ending. A laugh, after all, could end with a breath. Any moment. But now, I am realizing why the ending may have worked. Uncle Dick influenced my life, in fact, may have even saved it. But it was a tenuous rescue—after all, he was not there regularly, or reliably. Just enough to let me know such vitality, such joy in life, such humor and élan, were possible.

In 1988 I wrote him again. Told him how much his visits had meant, how important he had been to me. That I wrote poetry, taught it. He responded, and we began corresponding. My father had died in 1987, and in the spring of 1989 my mother and I flew to Guadalajara to find Uncle Dick. He was buoyant as ever, although almost blind. The conversation (how could talk with Dick be called a conversation? Like calling a butterfly a bug, a painted bunting a bird) scintillated, bounced, danced off the windows of the chauffeured car. The jacaranda was in full violet bloom. My mother took snapshots of Uncle Dick and me talking together, our faces turned to each other, mine a much younger, female version of his, the same long, large nose, the same pale, twinkling eyes. We laughed and laughed that visit, the first, and the last. He died a year later, in 1990, after cataract surgery had left him blind. But I have his final finished painting right here beside me on the wall as I write, a three-by-four foot riot of color that fuels my days.

❖ ONCE MORE, SQUAM LAKE ❖

The Poem

ONCE MORE, SQUAM LAKE

The lake whitens in the hot light
of July. At Sandy Beach we see the sunfish
circling their eggs, rippling the water.
The sunfish do what they've done before,
will do again. I sit in a haze

of sisters, nieces, mothers, grandmothers.
When I was seven, Old Jane Noble was Young
Jane Noble. When I was seventeen
she was one of the mothers who knitted
argyles on the playhouse porch.

Too hot today for socks, for knitting.
But tonight the loons will yodel
and last week they counted
nine new chicks, three more than last year.
My son is learning to fish the lake.

My father will teach him
to let the line fall quietly
(only a small furrow of water moving
beyond the nylon thread),
to hear where bass live, to find the depth

of the lake. I watch from the dock,
the lake takes the planks and rocks them
backward, forward, I forget
how old I am, what year it is,
how it all matters.

About the Writing

Augustus, in a red rental car, heading north on Interstate 93 after fly-
ing into Manchester. But this was the first time I did not stay on 93 all the
way to Squam Lake, to my mother's home in Center Sandwich, to friends
Daphne Mowatt and Jean Robinson, to Billy's General Store. A torrent of
memories that way: visceral tugs, and yet I was turning off, turning west
onto 89, to Hanover, and my mother's new home at Kendall Retirement
Community. My vision was blurry for about ten miles.

Since sometime in the early 1920s, my father's family had summered
at the Rockywold-Deephaven Camps on Squam Lake. In those days, fam-
ilies from East Coast cities from Baltimore to Boston arrived in early June
to stay through August. The men could never stay the whole summer;
Boston commuters returned to the office during the week, joining their
wives, daughters, and sons—and/or brothers, sisters, parents, aunts,
uncles, grandmothers, nieces, nephews, grandchildren—on weekends. But
most managed a month in July or August for an extended stay with the
family.

Begun in 1897 by two intrepid women, Alice Mabel Bacon and Mary
Alice Armstrong, the Rockywold-Deephaven Camps were founded on the
principle that city-dwellers needed to nourish their spirits by camping in
the woods, removed from the clamor and clatter of the city. Originally,
vacationing urbanites were housed in tents, but within a few years, the two
women had built basic pine cottages to accommodate the visitors. Miss
Bacon had lived in Japan, and even today, one senses the influence of that
country's architecture in the camps' structures. Residents take meals in an
alcohol-free common dining room, where the food is sensible (some say
boring) and plentiful. Canoes are available for a fee. Outside every cottage
door is a dark green ice box refilled daily with glacial chunks cut from the
lake in February. Until recently, all drinks were cooled with that ice, but
now, with the lake's water no longer safe to drink, the ice is used only for
chilling this proto-refrigerator, large enough for vacationers to store milk,
soft drinks, but little else, since cottages contain no cooking facilities. But
even though the lake water is no longer pure, and cottages are furnished
with electricity, bathrooms, and hot running water, the character of the
camps remains. Phone calls can be made only from the office or pay
phones in a public area. Cars are parked only in certain areas and quiet
times are observed. Residents participate in loon counts and mountain

hikes. And although most people now stay only a week or two, the camps are imbued with a sense of continuity, of history, of families come together in what former Director Frank Perkins called "our spirit's home."

I was born in September, 1942, shortly after my parents left Deephaven (there is a strong rivalry between Rockwold and "Deep," and my family had always been "Deep" people) for the season and returned to Summit, New Jersey, from which my father and grandfather commuted into New York. Summers we returned, along with many of the same families. As a toddler and pre-schooler, I watched my grandfather play horseshoes with his friends; I watched my father play tennis with his. I sat with my mother and grandmother and their friends and learned to knit. Later my grandfather taught me how to paddle a canoe, and he and my grandmother taught my sister Liza and me how to play canasta. Liza and I danced in the playhouse on Friday night during the children's hour for dancing; we swayed and sashayed to our own internal drummers and nobody minded. Sunday evenings we gathered at Flagstaff Point for vespers and sang "Now the day is over, night is drawing nigh, / Shadows of the evening steal across the sky."

After my parents moved us to Phoenix the summer of 1947, we sometimes flew back east in the summer and spent a couple of weeks at Squam. Waking up with the sun on my cot I was entirely happy, my mind free from its usual clotted worries and tangled fears. But around the time I was thirteen, probably for economic reasons (transporting a family of five back and forth across the country every summer would have been ridiculously expensive) we no longer made the pilgrimage at all. We took our annual two-week vacation at Oceanside, California, or in the White Mountains of Arizona, a nuclear family of five, crowded into the car and a cheap cabin.

The lake, with its Thoreauvian peace and Alcottian family warmth, might as well have drifted into the Atlantic. I was left with snapshots in my album, and a sense of loss so primal and powerful I could not give it words. I attended thirteen different schools in twelve years; we lived in thirteen different houses or apartments in my nineteen years of living "at home." And after I married, we moved even more, inhabiting sixteen places in thirty-six years.

But some time after my son was born, friends mentioned to my parents they had just returned from an idyllic two weeks in a rural spot that seemed untouched by time. It was pretty basic, they said, bad mattresses, mediocre cafeteria-style food, plain pine cottages, but so peaceful and beautiful they planned to return. My mother and father held their breaths.

Could the Rockywold-Deephaven Camps have survived? Not have sold off their extensive valuable lakefront footage? My parents were soon not only breathing but planning. The following summer they returned, to be welcomed by old friends (and their grown children and grandchildren), and the summer after that, they managed to bring all three daughters and our families back for two weeks.

The lake, shimmering in the sun and shifting under clouds, changing every moment of the day, had not changed. On the dock of the cottage called El Dorado (which still held my grandfather's shaving mirror nailed to the wall), the lake's rhythms lapped through my marrow. I had rocked on this spot from within my mother's womb, during the summer of 1942.

And now my four-year-old son was here, along with my sister Liza and her family and my sister Trisha. Jane Noble (known as a child as "Bitsy" because her mother was also Jane—later they were differentiated by the monikers "Big Jane" and "Little Jane"), whom I remembered as being years older than I, was here with her husband and children, and I found, to my amazement, that we were not separated by many years at all. Together we reconstructed stories of our grandparents' generation. My father helped my son catch the biggest bass of the year until some darned newcomer beat him by a quarter of an inch.

How could I not write this poem? I drafted it in 1982, during one of our return trips to Squam. This first draft, included here, is, like so many of mine, a flabby scrawl in much need of tightening and shaping. But most of the poem is already there, except for the ending, which took actually years to find. My old friend Kevin Clark was the one who showed me the way to the poem's ending. Through many revisions, the poem had concluded:

> I watch from the dock,
> the lake takes the planks and rocks them
> backward, forward, I forget
> how old I am, what year it is,
> it doesn't matter.

Kevin said the ending needed a surprise. And I began to realize that the last clause could follow as another in the series of direct objects for the verb "forget." To say "I forget" that "it doesn't matter" is contrary to the point of the poem. But by ending the poem with the line "how it all matters," the poem can suggest two things: one, that, here at the lake, I can forget how everything seems to matter, and, two, that I know how much everything does actually matter, as if exclaiming, "How it all matters!" To end this poem on a paradox still strikes me as just right.

I am not sure this is a good poem. It took five years and twenty-six submissions before Elinor Benedict of *Passages North*, accepted it. But even now, it makes me happy. It reminds me of the possibility of being entirely in the moment, lost in the dazzle of light on water, and at the same time keenly aware of all that came before us, that will follow us, that surrounds us. It reminds me how much my father adored my son and my son adored his grandfather, and how the tenderness of that relationship made up for much of my father's distance and indifference during most of my life. It reminds me that there was, even with all our moves and dislocations, one place on this earth that had always been home, that, I had had, unlike Edith Wharton's tragic character Lily Bart in *House of Mirth*, "one place dearer" than any other. In 1998, after I divorced my husband and started a fresh new life and home with my companion, I convinced Steve to accompany me to Squam Lake.

We canoed out to Loon Island and spent two days silently paddling in and out of coves, picking blueberries. In my mother's kitchen I made blueberry pie. We swam across Rattlesnake Cove and for the first time in my life, I, once the asthmatic, sickly member of the family, with Steve's encouragement, hiked Butterworth Trail, the steepest path up Rattlesnake Mountain. The following summer my son joined us, and we all three canoed through the Sandy Narrows into Peerface and True Coves. My father's ashes are scattered in that lake. Even in August, the water is cold, but whenever I have returned, the first thing I do is change into my swim suit and climb down the dock's rickety ladder into the lake. The sunfish have always been there.

But this past summer I was not driving to Squam. Even though for the past few years my mother has lived in the town of Center Sandwich, near, but not on, the water, visiting her has meant a return to the lake, a pilgrimage to Squam. Now I was heading west to the town where, in 1987, my father died at Dartmouth's Hitchcock Hospital. Hanover is the town where my mother eventually will die. But at eighty-four she is thriving in her new life at Kendall, and one of her oldest friends from Squam Lake, Jean Robinson, is one of the residents. Maybe on another trip I will head north and visit the lake again. And maybe not. I may be starting to be able to forget how it all matters. Perhaps I have learned, after thirty different moves to thirty different residences during my less than sixty years, that the lake—that expansive blue stillness, that sense of at-homeness, at-one-ness—is not only Squam, but something that exists inside, what Linda Gregg calls "a resonant source" for poetry, even for, as she puts it, "what ever that part of us is we call the soul." Perhaps, like Dorothy's ability to click her ruby shoes and return to Kansas, it is something that has been with me all along.

❖ WHAT CEILINGS ❖

WHAT CEILINGS

> O, reason not the need!
> —*King Lear*

Descending from the cool
ceiling of an antique shop on Royal Street:
chandeliers—hundreds, crystal
petals, gardens, waterfalls, concentric
galaxies, light exploding
over dark wood, carved
jade, inlaid pearl, old
man asleep in a velvet chair.

On the street the wail of a lone
sax winds out of itself
until it seems we could leave
our constraining
joints, freed from sharp
angles, weight of the concrete,
and lift, cluster, dazzle,
like all this glass.

I remember my room as a child,
its single ceiling fixture
a plain glass square
barely covering two light bulbs,
their hard glare. From the window
I could see only empty sky, no trees
grown high enough to move
beyond that pane.

In Nova Scotia, authorities have condemned
the home of a man who keeps
pigeons, hundreds, in his garret.
He has long ago lost count,
has never minded the mess.
He leaves the windows open.
Four generations under his roof.
Family, he says, all he's got.

The sound of those wings
overhead, among the rafters, fluttering
his ceiling. The years of droppings
whitening the dark floor. Soft fiber
of nesting, soft rustling of wings.
Sounds from beyond the ceiling that could be
water bubbling, wine glasses
clinking, people murmuring of love.

10:30 a.m.   11/14/89

(1)

In New Orleans the bones can walk
out of their joints and bend, click,
~~and~~ dazzle the way the drops
of the crystal chandeliers of the antique
  · shops on Royal Street glitter, heavy
with glass. Inside, away from the shimmer
of a lone sax on the street
the eye cranes ~~up at the fixtures~~
~~hanging from the ceiling,~~
crystal, ~~drops~~ arranged in concentric
circles, ~~crystal drops like~~ lush
jewels that would fit on a plump bare
breast, ~~arranged to cascade~~
~~in an explosion of white light~~
from the ceiling over the dark
wood, the carvings, the inlays,
the old man snoring in the chair
by the door.

Fixture after fixture,
cascading light over
the table

His bones curl in as his head
bends to his breast ~~bone,~~ his breathing
rattles the polite silence
of the shop, where it does not seem
quite right to say, "just looking."
We cannot see his eyes as we leave,
the glass of the door rattling
as we close it behind us.

Chandeliers like hard rain on the roof.
A sax like a toddler's wail.
Where did these fixtures come from,
what changes in neighborhoods
have brought them here, lined up
like endangered creatures in a zoo,
specimens of a time when there
was room to roam through floors
of large houses dressed in skirts
that took up more room than any of us
~~have any more even in our biggest bathroom.~~

It feels good to walk down this street
with the music, we walk side by side
and the pace of our legs finds a mutal
rhtyhme. Beyond the railings upstairs
on these houses I can't see any higher,
the blare of the evening hides the night.

2.
What do we have to look up to.
In Tucson in the fifties
I remember the one squre
of frosted glass the hid
the two bulbs behind it.
They lit the whole room with its pale
blue walls, but cast a hard shadow.

1

When I trried to look out
the window, it showed only the clouds,
and telephone lines, not tops of trtees,
They hadn´t grown tall enough.

3.
On the radio I hear
of a man who keeps 300 pigeons
in his garret. In Nova Scotia,
and he doesn´t mind their mess.
The upstairs windows open, they can fly
ibn and out as they like, he always leavs leaves
them food, they have bred
four generations of pegeons now,
under his own roof., A couple of dozen
favorites he lets live
in the downstairs part of his house,
doesn´t mind cleaning
up after them, they are his family,
he says.

The soud of all those wings
overhead. The sense of the layers
of droppings (you just know he never cleaned),
building lioke layers of sculpture over the
hard wood florr of the attic, the nesting, the wings.

Once, years ago, when our son was a toddler,
the man next door began shooting
the puigoens that roosted on our roofs. Another
neighbor caught them when he could, in paper bags.
Once I let one go: the sound they made
was like water bubbling, like someone
saying, "that´s okay, hjoney, a comforting
chirring.

2

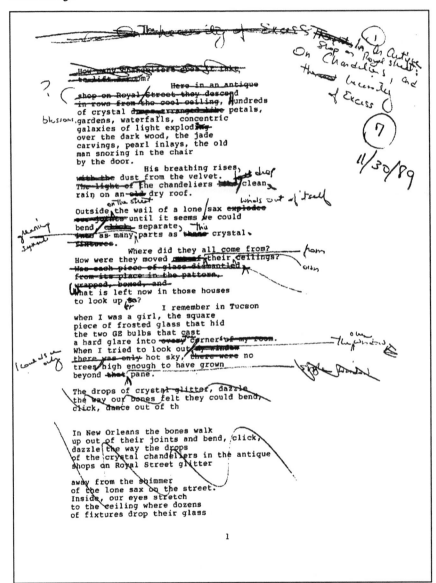

The [?]ity of Excess

How many chandeliers does it take,
to lift a room?

Here in an antique
shop on Royal Street they descend
in rows from the cool ceiling, hundreds
of crystal drops arranged like petals,
blossoms, gardens, waterfalls, concentric
galaxies of light exploding
over the dark wood, the jade
carvings, pearl inlays, the old
man snoring in the chair
by the door.   His breathing rises,
with the dust from the velvet.
The light of the chandeliers like clean,
rain on an old dry roof.
on the street
Outside, the wail of a lone sax explodes
our joints until it seems we could
bend, click, separate, this
into as many parts as these crystal
fixtures.

Where did they all come from?   from
How were they moved out of their ceilings?
Was each piece of glass dismantled,
from its place in the pattern,
wrapped, boxed, and
What is left now in those houses
to look up so?

I remember in Tucson
when I was a girl, the square
piece of frosted glass that hid
the two GE bulbs that cast
a hard glare into every corner of my room.
When I tried to look out my window
there was only hot sky, there were no
trees high enough to have grown
beyond that pane.

The drops of crystal glitter, dazzle
the way our bones felt they could bend,
click, dance out of th

In New Orleans the bones walk
up out of their joints and bend, click,
dazzle the way the drops
of the crystal chandeliers in the antique
shops on Royal Street glitter

away from the shimmer
of the lone sax on the street.
Inside, our eyes stretch
to the ceiling where dozens
of fixtures drop their glass

1

7
11/30/89

Once, years ago, the man next door began shooting
the pigeons that roosted on our roofs. Another
neighbor caught them when he could, in paper bags.
Once, angry for the birds, having grown
fond of their presence, I let one go: the sound it made
was like water bubbling, like glass
tearing, like cascades of wings
refracted far overhead, flying
into light.

4

WHAT CEILINGS

> "O reason not the need. . . ."
>   --King Lear

[handwritten: Lawrence says no]

Descending from the cool
ceiling of an antique shop on Royal
Street: chandeliers, hundreds, crystal
petals, gardens, waterfalls, concentric
galaxies of light exploding
over the dark wood, the carved
jade, inlaid pearl, old
man ~~dozing~~ by the door.   *[handwritten: stet ? / Cushed on a chair]*

On the street the wail of a lone
sax winds out of itself
until it seems we could leave
our constraining
joints, freed from sharp
angles, weight of the concrete,
and lift, cluster, dazzle,
like all this glass. *[handwritten: Wesy says yes to this change]*

I remember my room as a child, the single
square of frosted glass with two timid
curls etched into the sides. That fixture
barely hid its 60 watt bulbs, their hard
glare.   From the window
I could see only empty sky, no trees
had grown high enough to move
beyond that pane.

In Nova Scotia, authorities have condemned
the home of a man who keeps
pigeons, hundreds, in his garret.
He says he has long ago lost count,
has never minded the mess. He leaves
the windows open. They have bred
four generations under his roof.
His family, he says, they're all he's got.

The sound of all those wings
overhead, among the rafters, fluttering
his ceiling. The years of droppings
whitening the dark floor. The soft fiber
of nesting, soft rustling of wings.
Sounds from beyond the ceiling that could be
water bubbling, wine glasses
clinking, people murmuring of love.

                                   Wendy Barker

[handwritten top right: 12 / 12/7/89 / Writers Workshop]

Revision, Denise Levertov's Comments

Denise Levertov – 4/7/90

I like this (as well as I like it)

WHAT CEILINGS

"O reason not the need. . . ."
--King Lear

Descending from the cool
ceiling of an antique shop on Royal
Street: chandeliers--hundreds, crystal
petals, gardens, waterfalls, concentric
galaxies, light exploding
over dark wood, carved
jade, inlaid pearl, old
man asleep in a velvet chair.

On the street the wail of a lone
sax winds out of itself
until it seems we could leave
our constraining
joints, freed from sharp
angles, weight of the concrete,
and lift, cluster, dazzle,
like all this glass.

I remember my room as a child, the ceiling's
single square of plain glass, faint
curls etched on the edges. That fixture
barely hid the 60 watt bulb, hard
glare. From the window
I could see only empty sky, no trees
grown high enough to move
beyond that pane.

In Nova Scotia, authorities have condemned
the home of a man who keeps
pigeons, hundreds, in his garret.
He has long ago lost count,
has never minded the mess.
He leaves the windows open.
Four generations under his roof.
Family, he says, all he's got.

The sound of all those wings
overhead, among the rafters, fluttering
his ceiling. The years of droppings
whitening the dark floor. Soft fiber
of nesting, soft rustling of wings.
Sounds from beyond the ceiling that could be
water bubbling, wine glasses
clinking, people murmuring of love.

I'd like to see another word (transparency?) in stanza 2, or else in stanza 3 (single square window? with 'plain' affixed to 'fixture'?) rather than the repetition.

Wendy Barker

About the Writing

The epigraph for this poem is one of the most moving lines in English literature. In Act II, Scene iv of Shakespeare's *King Lear*, the covetous, heartless Goneril and Regan strip their father of each of his retainers, asking, "What need you five and twenty? ten? or five?" and finally, "What need one?" The response from the heartbroken Lear is a powerful question applicable far beyond the scope of the play: "O, reason not the need!"

What a plea this is. How do we count what counts in our lives? Why do we need our knickknacks, our tchotchkies, our *objets d'art?* Our vases, candlesticks, bracelets, photos, and embroidered pillows? Why do we need even books? What need a hundred, or fifty, or twenty? They kill trees, their production pollutes the environment, and they require time and effort to store, organize, and dust. The money my companion and I have spent on bookcases to house our collections could feed a family in rural Pakistan for a year, maybe two. Why not just find things online? Why not use a library?

"O, reason not the need." I cherish our books, relish being able to turn to a volume, as I just did, to look up a passage. To re-imprint half-familiar utterances in the mind. To remember, to find again, or to find for the first time. Like living with voices, other lives, friends, companions of the mind, who speak to us as soon as we open the door of a book's cover. Even the covers, or the flyleaves inside, often speak, causing us to remember the circumstances of a volume's purchase—a particular city block, a friend. Books themselves comprise a retinue of sorts, attendants for the mind. Books are my luxuries.

But are they luxuries? Or necessities? Are bangles for a South Indian dancer only luxuries? Are dozens of tubes of oil paint for an artist? Does a piano need more than twelve keys? Sure, a dozen notes can make music— but with eighty-eight keys, how many more possibilities! Are desires for such plenty frivolous? Or manifestations of the human spirit, of the yearning to transcend this "mortal coil"?

I do not remember which came first, my hearing the story on NPR of the Nova Scotian and his pigeons or my first trip to New Orleans. During the fall of 1989, the two formed a mental connection I could not sever. Was the desire for an attic filled with fluttering pigeons, I wondered, that different from the desire for a ceiling hung with glittering chandeliers? The images obsessed me until the chandeliers were cooing and the doves clinking and dazzling.

Listening to the car radio, returning home after taking my son to a school rehearsal, I was struck by the Canadian's plight, by the fact that his house had been condemned. When asked by the interviewer about the birds, he explained he did not mind their droppings. The pigeons were his only family; generations had bred beneath his roof. He knew each bird individually. Suddenly another memory entered the car: years before, during the seventies, while my husband, son, and I lived in Berkeley, pigeons (which can also be called "rock doves") began roosting on the rooftops in our neighborhood.

I loved their cooings and murmurings, the sounds of their wings. But the neighbors talked about shooting them, and began, actually, to trap them. Our roofs would be permanently damaged, they warned. Of course they were right. But to me the birds seemed a visitation, a gift, almost a kind of annunciation. About a year after writing "What Ceilings," I wrote the poem "Annunciations," which I later included in *Way of Whiteness*. Its first section goes like this:

> The day the doves began to roost on her roof.
> Their curdled calls, a sound of something boiling.
> Odd, the fog that crept so cool, mornings, around the windows,
> that by noon cleared for only a couple of hours,
> returning mid-afternoon to blanket the house
> so the murmuring of the doves seemed louder.
>
> She refilled the feeder that hung
> outside the kitchen window. The rush
> of tiny kernels of millet into the long tube.
> Rush of the small wings of finches, chickadees
> landing on the metal rods. When the doves flew down,
> smaller birds, frightened, flew away.
>
> Neighbors fussed about the doves, too many,
> they tore the roofs. The couple next door trapped them.
> Evenings she would creep outside, let the birds loose.
> Would come back into the lighted house, finish
> the dishes, place them, dripping, into the white drainer
> as the doves fluttered into place

under her eaves, settled on her roof, quiet now,
so all she could hear as she slept were the fog horns
calling from the wet black bay, the fog horns,
their low, incessant calling.

The "she" in the poem is being asked to move beyond her present state—
she hears something the neighbors do not. They are cognizant only of
pests—but the woman is feeding them, freeing them, aware she is being
called to something unknown to her.

"What Ceilings" expresses a similar awareness. Like the saxophone's
lone wail that "winds out of itself / until it seems we could leave / our con-
straining / joints," the poem is about that desire to go beyond the bound-
aries of self, to merge with something beyond us. And it is a poem
extolling the virtues of excess, of surrendering to something overwhelm-
ing, the way we do in sex, the arts, or religious ecstasy.

The same fall I heard about the Nova Scotian and his pigeons, I spent
a few days in New Orleans while attending a conference. I had never been
to the Crescent City before, and, in the company of several other poets,
found the French Quarter mesmerizing. Down every street floated the mel-
low, fluid notes of a saxophone and the hypnotic rhythms of drums.
Everyone seemed to be strolling with a loose-limbed walk, legs ready to
dance. And Royal Street! My friends—poet Peter Cooley among them—
poked into antique shop after shop, patient with each other's lingering
over mahogany highboys, brocaded loveseats, and gilt-handled vases.

Looking up at the ceiling of one shop, I could barely bring my focus
back down. Row after row of elaborate chandeliers lined the store's ceil-
ing, and I was transported. The music, the friends, the beauty—all con-
tributed to a sense of near transcendence.

What is a ceiling, anyway? That which covers us, shelters us? Or that
which sets our limits, as in the phrase "glass ceiling," which suggests a bar-
rier to further growth? But a ceiling composed of crystal drops, of shim-
mering spiraling branches and intricate leaves, a ceiling cascading rivulets
of glass seemed a dissolving of limits, as if the solid plane directly above
us had melted into water, dissolved into light. Like an attic filled with birds
flying out and in, this ceiling seemed to lift me, until I could leave behind
old constraints, ordaining myself "loos'd of imaginary limits and lines," as
Walt Whitman declared in "Song of the Open Road."

The poem went through sixteen drafts before I began submitting it to
journals. I brought the poem to my senior-level poetry workshop, to my

poetry group, and also received helpful comments from Pat Mora. When Denise Levertov visited in April 1990, she, too, commented, writing "I like this (I like it I like it!)." Her suggestions helped especially with the third stanza, which describes the stark, constraining ceiling of my childhood bedroom in Tucson, and I was finally able to clarify that troublesome section. I sent the poem to seven journals, and, within a year and a half, Jerry Bradley of the *New Mexico Humanities Review* accepted it. For several years, "What Ceilings" was the title poem of the manuscript-in-progress that became *Way of Whiteness.* While organizing that collection, I removed "What Ceilings," deciding that its theme was better expressed in other poems. Now, I think I was wrong; I wish I had kept it in the book.

This is not a poem calling for increased consumption of material goods. It is a poem about opening out to a luxurious "house" of the mind. "I dwell in Possibility— / A fairer House than Prose," wrote Emily Dickinson. A poem comes to us, says Stanley Kunitz, "like rapture breaking on the mind." Rapture: an attic of rustling doves, a ceiling of luminous crystal drops—"people murmuring of love."

❖ CUMULUS AND CIRRUS ❖

❖ CUMULONIMBUS INCUS ❖

CUMULUS AND CIRRUS

About such majesty
they were dead on, those Old
Masters of the page-long
paragraph with parentheticals,
semi-colons, punctuation
marks as spirals, curlicues,
and always, the light
behind the foaming flesh
of turbulence, perhaps
even a god in the air.

The Poem

CUMULONIMBUS INCUS

Build-up of white
turret upon white, but wait—
half-way, dark, there:
a wedge, break, em-dash—
pause in the tumult as
warm air cools, takes
a breath, forms a second-
story floor, shift in the plot,
new base for the chapter's
finale, moist hot risings
to hammer the storm.

7-31-00

CUMULUS AND CIRRUS

About such majesty,
They were dead on;
those old Masters
of the page by
paragraph little parallel tile,
semi-colons. [struck out]
spiral,
penetration
makes as spirals, curlicues,
and always the light
behind the foaming flush
of turbulence in the air.

Handwritten First Draft

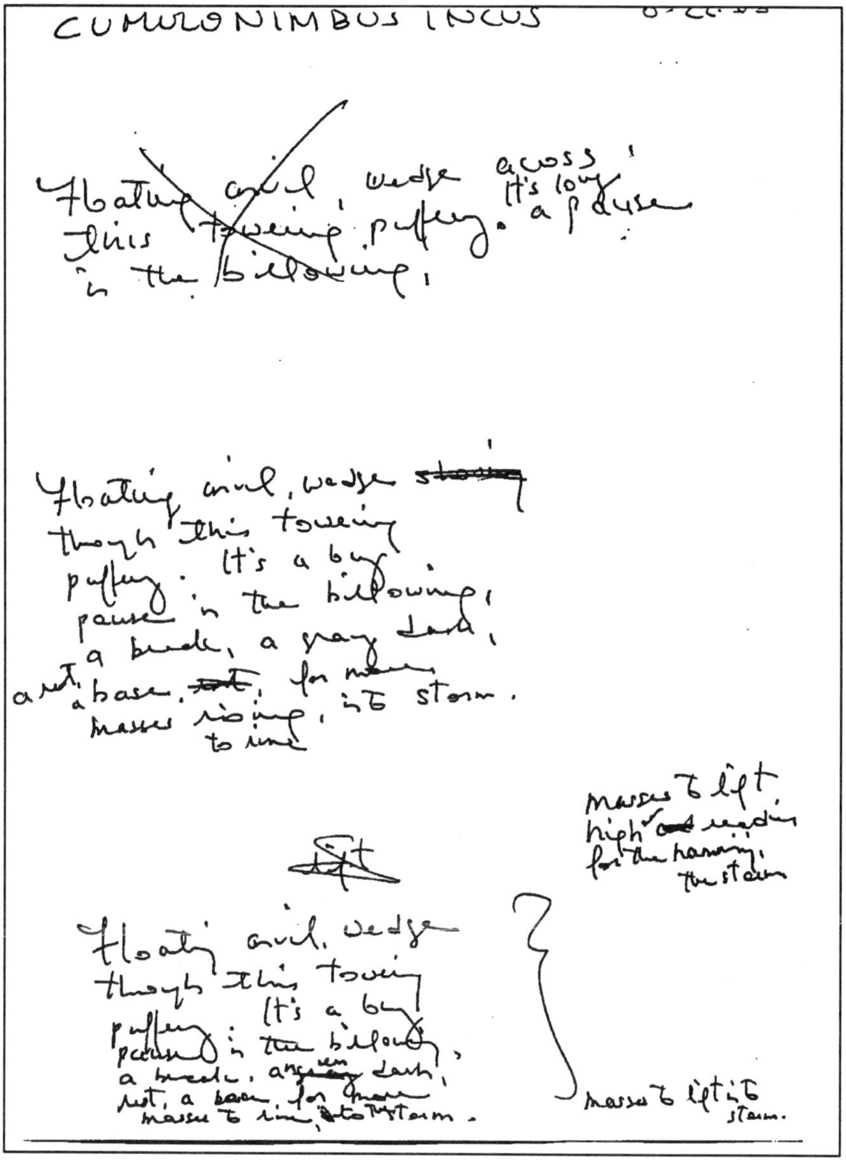

CUMULONIMBUS INCUS

Floating anvil, wedge across
This towering puffing. It's long a pause
in the billowing,

Floating anvil, wedge ~~storing~~
through this towering
puffing. It's a big
pause in the billowing,
a break, a gray ~~dark~~,
a rest, a base. ~~rest~~, for more
masses rising, into storm.
to rise

masses to lift,
high ~~and~~ reading
for the hammering,
the storm

~~lift~~ Sit

Floating anvil, wedge
through this towering
puffing. It's a big
pause in the billowing,
a break, an ~~gray~~ dark,
rest, a base for more
masses to rise, into the storm.

masses to lift into storm.

G rowing up in Arizona, I was often happiest doing one of two things: reading, or lying on the grass, and looking up at clouds. I was a lonely kid. But I loved the sky.

In summertime Tucson, the morning's cumulus puffs swelled steadily into dense, towering cumulonimbus structures that filled most of the sky, so that by four-thirty or five in the afternoon the rain pelted down, cooling us by ten or fifteen degrees. Sometimes a thunderstorm caught my sisters and me still lolling around the neighborhood pool. Reluctantly we grabbed our towels and headed for home, our rubber thongs squeaking and squishing in the fast-rising puddles, the shirts over our suits soaked through to our sunburned skin. Sometimes the roaring and flashing of thunder and lightning would continue after dark, and sometimes, sometimes, if we were really lucky, the electricity went out. Dinner in the dark was thrilling; brushing our teeth by candlelight even better. I doubt if our parents shared our disappointment when, suddenly, occasionally with a little click, all the lights popped back on again and the corners of rooms assumed their usual brightly-lighted angles.

Even as an adult, I have found what newscasters call "weather events" engrossing. I actually like the Weather Channel, a predilection that has resulted in much teasing. When I have admitted my obsession with swirling graphic representations of storm fronts, I have received hoots of derision. Like watching paint dry, some have said. Even my patient, considerate companion rushes past the Weather Channel as fast as his fingers can click the remote.

But I want to linger. Cloud formations, levels of humidity, temperatures, flooding, and drought: are not these the raw stuff from which our lives are made? All of us, human and non-human, are dependent upon the weather. Too cold, people die. Too wet, trees rot. And is weather not also intricately connected with our moods, our tantrums, calms, and exuberances? "What a beautiful day!" we exclaim to one another, not bothering to notice how the atmospheric pressure has risen and the humidity has dropped.

Maybe it was out of sheer stubbornness that I began, about a year ago, to write poems about weather. Maybe I just finally acknowledged my genuine curiosity. I bought field guides to weather. I studied cloud formations. While driving I was no longer bored. Not only could my eye linger on shapes and colors and shades of clouds, but I could tell whether I was viewing Cirrus Uncinus or Cumulus Mammatus. I often struggle to remember details others seem to find important—names of basketball players, movie stars, political leaders—but weather became my subject, and I took a perverse delight in pointing out atmospheric formations to friends: "Ah! Look at those Crepuscular Rays!" "Wow! Cirrocumulus Undulatus."

The first weather poem I wrote did not focus on any phenomenon with a Latin name. I wrote a poem I initially called "Rain," and then renamed "Downpour," simple enough terms in anyone's vocabulary. I have now written two dozen poems (with the same number in various stages of revision or abandonment) about weather and clouds. This series, with which I have been obsessed for over a year, began because I was stuck in the rain.

I had been visiting my mother in New Hampshire and was scheduled to take the bus to Greenfield, Massachusetts, where the host for my evening poetry reading was to pick me up and take me to her house and then to the reading. But the bus company had changed the drop-off point, and instead of being let out at the supermarket on the outskirts of town where my host had said she would meet me, three other passengers and I were dropped off at the town square. Thunderheads had been building all afternoon, and by the time I retrieved my bag from the underbelly of the bus, the sky had opened. The four of us were drenched in the ninety seconds it took to drag our suitcases to the sidewalk. There was no sheltered area. The huge leafy branches of old trees helped somewhat, but they also contributed to the water that dripped onto and from our noses, our sleeves. I managed to find my weather-proof parka from my bag and put it on. It was soaked in seconds. The rain was so intense we could barely see five feet in front of us. But I did spot pay phones, and called my host: I left a message on her machine, but, obviously, she was waiting for me at the supermarket several miles away.

She arrived after about an hour. I was surprised I never panicked. I knew she would find me, and she did. I also counted on a hot bath before the poetry reading. In her warm, dry car, she showered me with apologies. I was fine, I said, I just needed to take a hot bath and change into a dry skirt and blouse. Her face grew red; we don't have time, she said, I have to drive you straight to the reading.

By the time we arrived at the neighboring town's book store for the reading, I was somewhat dry, but chilled and rumpled. Still, I did the reading, and no one seemed to mind—or notice—my dishevelment. The next day, after a deep sleep in a good bed after a hot shower, I started jotting in my journal on the bus to Boston. I had not allowed myself to write experimentally for many months, and soon the pen began moving as if by itself.

Returning home, I titled the new poem "Downpour." It was quickly followed by others, and soon I was immersed in guide books to weather phenomena, observing types of clouds I had never noticed. As the summer progressed, early evening walks often resulted in new cloud poems.

"Cumulus and Cirrus" was written after witnessing a particularly lavish and brilliant evening sky, so filled with various shapes (made only of water and ice particles, I reminded myself), I felt I was in the midst of a Renaissance painting. I know not all readers will recognize that the poem's first two lines play on W. H. Auden's "Musée des Beaux Arts," with its resonant lines: "About suffering they were never wrong, / The Old Masters: how well they understood...." But I hope readers who do know the poem will immediately sense something of the layers I am trying to convey, that the visual presence of this particular South Texas sky seemed to transcend oceans and centuries. In his poem, Auden refers to Brueghel's painting of *The Fall of Icarus*, who, flying too close to the sun, was burned and fell back to the earth. Auden comments that everything "turns away / Quite leisurely from the disaster." Although the "ploughman may / Have heard the splash, the forsaken cry" of Icarus, he ploughs on: "for him it was not an important failure." While suffering the ultimate punishment for trying to reach too far, the dying Icarus in Brueghel's painting is not even noticed.

But I am twisting Auden's lines: in my short poem it is "majesty," not "suffering," about which the "Old Masters" painted, and I say they were "dead on," a colloquial way of saying they were, as Auden put it, "never wrong." Using "dead" in such a slangy way is also a subtle way of hinting that this entire scene of tumultuous clouds might be "dead" in the sense that its glorious effect is even more dated in this era of media sound-bites and clipped clichés than the elaborate prose style of someone like, say, Henry James, with his "page-long / paragraph[s] with parentheticals." It is too lushly beautiful, too aesthetically charged, too extravagant a scene even to exist right above the WalMart and the freeway. It is as if the sky dropped down from the world of Auden, James, the Old Masters, even from the ancient world. Yet, I was walking right under it, an amazing experience, almost as if the gods from ancient Rome might have returned, as if Jupiter himself might be lurking behind one of these grandiose visual manifestations of moist air. This is "majesty," not "suffering," and I am doing my best to be, unlike the ploughman in Brueghal's painting, a witness to the moment. But the poem just hints at all this, a fleeting impression, before it, like the majestic scene itself, is over.

"Cumulus and Cirrus" all but wrote itself. But "Cumulonimbus Incus" stuttered and staggered through several dozen drafts. I was at first intrigued by the fact that *incus* in Latin means "anvil," and that the sometimes visible wedge formed in the midst of a huge cumulonimbus cloud structure can be the base from which the final flourishing cloud tower rises, almost invariably resulting in a severe thunderstorm. I kept playing with the anvil image. The poem originally began

Floating anvil, a wedge
through the pillowy
swells.

But the friends who read the early drafts were confused. Reluctantly, I gave up on using the word "anvil." Several drafts later, I gave up on another metaphorical hobby horse I had been riding. As I had in done in "Cumulus and Cirrus," I was trying to compare the cloud type with a grammatical pattern requiring a particular kind of punctuation. I had begun describing this formation by saying it was composed of complex sentences, "Clause after clause." Finally I cut the clauses completely. Although I retained the em-dash in line four, I decided to think beyond grammar, and allow the poem to go further. As I let go of that earlier idea, I suddenly thought of the incus as "a second- / story floor, shift in the plot, / new base for the chapter's / finale."

These poems have a happy ending; shortly before leaving for Bulgaria in September 2000, I sent them, on a hunch, to Joseph Parisi, the editor of *Poetry*. He took them. And *Poetry Daily* then picked them up to run online at www.poems.com. I like these poems. They allow me to draw sap from the roots of the Romantic poets, who, even in our post-post modern era, still influence me. And I like what I do to write these poems, which is to take long walks, look up, let go of myself, and breathe the air. If, unlike Wordsworth, I cannot wander "lonely as a cloud" near an entire field of daffodils, I can at least observe the phenomena of clouds. I can at least allow manifestations of the non-human world to "flash upon that inward eye / Which is the bliss of solitude." Right now, I am devouring Richard Hamblin's *The Invention of Clouds*, the story of the man who, around the time Wordsworth published the Preface to *Lyrical Ballads*, first classified cloud formations and gave them their Latin names. These days I have left off mining my own past and memories, except in some of these essays; right now, I have my head in the clouds.

❖ SWALLOW WATCHER ❖

SWALLOW WATCHER

Every house needs someone to watch the swallows,
someone willing
to half close the eyes, lean the head back
against a tall chair
in a garden, on a porch, in a courtyard.

It doesn't matter if a cheap paperback
falls wrinkled from the knees,
a wine glass dangles
empty from the hand.
What matters is the watching:
                                    following

the lifts and darts
of the small birds,
the racings and screechings over territory,
the jags and dips for insects,
the gliding on wind.

About the time
the neighbor's porch light comes on
and the sky
can't hold color any more
the swallow watcher moves inside

to the glare of living room lights,
but he turns, leans
against the cool glass of the sliding door,
and stares out at the dark sifting down,
quiet as feathers, as wings.

Draft

```
SWALLOW WATCHER


Every house needs someone to watch the swallows,
somebody willing
to half close the eyes, lean the head back
against a tall chair
in a garden, on a porch, in a courtyard.

It doesn't matter whether a cheap paperback
falls wrinkled from the knees,
a glass of wine dangles
empty from the hand.
What matters is the watching:

following the lifts and darts
of the small birds,
the racings and screechings over territory,
the jags and dips for insects,
the gliding on wind.

The brittle cheeping in the summer chimney
begins about the time
the neighbor's porch comes on,
about the time the sky can't hold
color any more . . .

about the time the swallow watcher
turns and comes inside
to the glare of the living room lights,
blink and turns again
lean against the cool glass of the sliding door,

and stares out at the dark,
at the dark rising, light as swallows' feathers.
```

9

About the Writing

J une in San Antonio can be luscious—wildflowers a kaleidoscope swirling across empty fields, mesquite and oak leaves still gleaming and fresh. The sun has not yet scorched and exhausted us, as it will by August. In June of 1984, I was teaching a first-session summer-school graduate class in poetry. It was not creative writing, but a course in the genre of poetry, and included poets I most loved, such as Donne, Keats, Dickinson, Yeats, and Stevens. This is still, seventeen years later, one of my favorite courses.

And I taught it that June at night. I had much of the day for myself and my family, with plenty of time to prepare for the class before leaving for the university around five. The house we lived in during that time perched on an uphill slope above the road. We propped our feet on the wooden rail of the back deck and watched the cars go by, the dogs cavorting, the birds flitting. About five, the swallows would start to circle, to dip and dart, catching insects as they readied to settle for the night.

Often when I left the house, my husband would be tilted back in his chair, his wine glass in his hand and a half-empty bottle and the dogs at his feet. He would stay on the deck till the sky turned dark, till the cicadas began their ratcheting percussion. One evening, as I pulled into our university's parking lot, the scene I had just left at home resonated so vividly I could not open the car door. It was a mood I could not leave, a haloed moment I refused to let pass. I wrote the poem on the backs of deposit slips while sitting in the hot car and was fifteen minutes late to my class.

I was not thinking about writing a poem as I drove to the campus, but about D. H. Lawrence, whose poems I had been preparing to teach earlier in the day. I was haunted by the opening of "Bavarian Gentians," which begins:

> Not every man has gentians in his house
> in soft September, at slow, sad Michaelmas.

Suddenly, "not every" became "every," and the first line wrote itself: "Every house needs someone to watch the swallows."

As much as I enjoyed teaching, and as much as I enjoyed teaching this graduate course in poetry, I had not wanted to leave home that evening. But leaving a leisurely summer twilight was made easier because the "swallow watcher" remained, even as I left. If I could not be there, watching the birds dip and the evening darken, at least my husband could be. But under the surface of the poem also lies a deep sense of pain. For years I had been tearing myself away from my young son in order to commute to graduate school—and now once again, I could not stay home to enjoy the evening with my family. I had to teach.

I was about to enter a classroom illuminated by fluorescent glare, about to engage in discussions about words for three hours. I loved words, and I thoroughly enjoyed that group of students. Yet for so much of my life, I had been interrupted while immersed in moments of what Lawrence called "wise passiveness," a concept not unlike Keats' notion of "negative capability." I wanted to be the one who could remain watching the swallows; I wanted to stay immersed in that moment. But in actuality I was also the swallow watcher, watching both the swallows and my husband watching them. Like the speaker in Walt Whitman's "Song of Myself," I was "both in and out of the game."

> For the wonder that bubbles into my soul,
> I would be a good fountain,

says Lawrence in "The Song of a Man Who Has Come Through." He ends this poem:

> What is the knocking?
> What is the knocking at the door in the night?
> It is somebody wants to do us harm.
>
> No, no, it is the three strange angels.
> Admit them, admit them.

In writing the poem, I did the admit the "angels." Even though the moment in "real time" with the birds and the evening was abbreviated, I had let the whole poem in. I expressed my longing to remain on the deck poised between house and ground and sky, between daytime and nighttime, neither inside nor outside, on the threshold, the line separating me from the swallows and the dissolving sky.

But of course I could not dissolve, because I had to keep living, and making a living. I had to meet the faces I was teaching. The delicious paradox is that although I had not wanted to be on campus that night, if I had not been meeting with a class of stimulating graduate students, I would never have written "Swallow Watcher." I see now how our reading for the course influenced the poem, for it contains echoes of Keats' "To Autumn," where gathering "swallows twitter in the skies," and Stevens' "Sunday Morning," where, "At evening, casual flocks of pigeons make / Ambiguous undulations as they sink, / Downward to darkness, on extended wings." And although I still think the rhythm is off in line 6 (I probably should have cut the modifier "cheap" before "paperback"), I am amazed to find this is one poem of mine I still like reading.

❖ PICNIC MAKINGS ❖

PICNIC MAKINGS

Fourth grade cafeteria lunches. If you
brought your own you sat on the floor.
A sea of crowded children. I'd look inside
my paper bag for the cookies and sandwich:
cheese, or baloney, or peanut butter and
jelly on a good day. Sucking the last
bit of milk at the bottom of the carton.

*

When we dated, I would ask him, could we
stop to eat, and he would always say "Sure,
how about here," swing his bright white Healey
into the nearest drive-in. He'd always be ready
to eat, or cook, and even baked the first time
I stayed with him in his trailer. Made me
oatmeal raisin cookies, a double recipe.

*

In Guadalajara my uncle showed us around.
He knew just where to eat, knew the owners.
In the streets he cried, Look, people
are eating wherever they like, they simply
sit down on a curb with their lunch, eat
together right here in the square,
in Guadalajara it is always a picnic!

*

On the train we ate on the pull-down table,
I trimmed green onions with an army knife,
we shared a quiche we had bought in Chartres.
Cherries. We gathered the pits into a kleenex.
The train swayed from side to side, rocking,
we had the whole compartment to ourselves,
and finished two bottles of wine, easy.

*

South Padre Island, the end of August.
On the sand you hold a spoon to my mouth,
soft white ice cream on the spoon. I take
the cold in my mouth, hold it on my tongue
before I swallow. You put your spoon back
into the cup, offer again, Would you like
some more? Here. Have some more.

Notes

THE PICNIC ISLAND

1.
Choose a tray for a picnic: wooden, red,
pink animals and birds carved

choose a tray for a small extravagance,
red, pink, brilliance to house
small bread, a dark purple plum.

It will be the picnic of a life
~~taking~~ time
for choosing ~~a~~ a purple

plum, just one, in the upper
right hand corner of the carved
wooden tray, a lean loaf,

the animals bray, silent,
the colors rock,
the train.

2.
~~On the~~
Once on the ~~tray~~ Train There can
be many picnics

Once on the tray there can be many
picnics

The animals walk two by Two
- the elephant and kangaroo

A plum can contain a picnic
can release a picnic
of wet dark seeds
scattered over a brick floor.

1

8/31/92

THE PICNIC ISLAND

1.
Fourth grade cafeteria lunches. Those of us
children who brought their own had to sit on the floor.
I would look inside my paper bag.
What kind of sandwich: cheese, baloney, peanut butter
and jelly on a good day.
Sucking the small bit of milk left at the bottom of the carton.

At home, was my mother in the kitchen, was the cold
tap running over hard potatoes that she would boil
later for the dinner I would have to wait for?

2.
When we dated, I would ask you, could we stop
to eat, and you would always say "Sure, how about
here," swing your bright white Healey
into the nearest drive-in. You'd always be ready
to eat, or cook, and even baked the first time
I came down to see you in the trailer where you lived.
You fed me cookies, oatmeal, a double recipe.

3.
On the train we eat on the pull-down table,
I trim green onions with an army knife, we share
a quiche we bought in Chartres. Cherries, so many
we lose count of the pits, gather them into a kleenex.
The train moves from side to side, rocking as it goes,
we have the whole compartment to ourselves,
finish two bottles of wine, easy.

4.
In Guadalajara my Uncle Dick the painter leads us around.
He knows just where to take us to eat, only the places
where they cook for gringo intestines,
and we eat everything on our plates.
But in the streets he cries constantly, Look, look
the people are eating wherever they like, they simply
sit down on a curb with their lunch, they eat together
right here in the square, in Guadalajara it is always a picnic.

5.

South Padre at the end of a long summer.
We drove down in a friend's Suburban she calls Moby Dick.
We arrived in the belly of her car, unloaded
our sacks of breads, long and round loaves, six of us
had brought for each other, raspberries and nuts,
green and yellow peppers, coffee, tea, juice, milk.

At the beach we could run along to try to find the end
of the horizon, the pale sand gleaming from left to right
as far as we could see, as far as we could run,
and the pale sea foaming and rocking in a clean stripe
above the sand as far left and far right as far as we could see
and when we walked out into the water it could have rocked
us on out, farther than we could go.

One afternoon you held out your spoon to my mouth,
soft ice cream on a spoon, and you held it while
it took the cool softness into my mouth and swallowed.
You put your spoon right back into the cup and
offered more, there was more, and there was enough.

About the Writing

Hot August right now, the heat made more oppressive by the knowledge that classes will soon begin again, along with committee meetings, phone calls, memos, and e-mail messages that often have the effect of creating guilt, guilt that I can never do enough. Always, classes could have been better prepared, my comments on returned essays could have been more helpful, and essays graded sooner. My office hours could have been longer, committee reports more detailed, recommendations more thorough.

Teaching is a profession with enormous rewards, but it can also be devouring. At times I have felt like a turkey carcass the day after Thanksgiving, and to protect my survival (for once I am not being metaphoric, but quite literal) I have had to learn just how much of myself I can offer to feed others, and how much to withhold, to keep for myself. I have had to learn to create firm boundaries, to know when to say, "I'm sorry, I can't make that meeting."

As I write this, I am preparing to return to the university after having been on leave for a year. I am afraid the banquet of open-ended time that has fed me will shrink, in an Alice-in-Wonderland metamorphosis, from a spacious room filled with long buffet tables of raspberry concoctions and buttermilk biscuits to an airline's plastic snack plate with a few sodden microwaved peas.

Time and food. Food, in time. "Picnic Makings" is about the relationship between the two. I wrote the poem in late August of 1992, after returning from a trip to South Padre Island with close friends. On the way down to the coast we passed field after field of blooming purple sage. The beach was white and clean, the ocean cool and uncluttered. On the way home, my friends pulled in at a Dairy Queen, a franchise I have never patronized, my health-food proclivities dominant even while on the road. My friends all ordered Blizzards, and began seducing me with spoonfuls of soft ice cream. They literally spoon-fed me, over and over, causing a rush of feeling so cared for, so loved, I was light-headed all the way back to San Antonio, and not just from the unfamiliar sugar high.

The poem's ending tries to express the feeling of that experience, but it does not describe the actual events of that August day. In reworking the poem, I realized that images of a Texas highway Dairy Queen would not convey the intensity of the pleasure, the lusciousness of savoring not only the sensuousness of the ice cream but also the generosity of the friends' offerings. I hoped by placing the poem's last section on the beach, and by specifically referring to South Padre Island, the poem would end with a sense of leisure, of sun, water, and sand, of spaciousness and possibility.

The poem's ending works in stark contrast to its beginning with "A sea of crowded children" at lunch in a school cafeteria, a meal time rushed and heavily supervised. "If you / brought your own you sat on the floor." Anything not institutionalized, anything of "your own" separated you from friends and relegated you to second-class citizenship. Even the lunch brought from home was limited to a single sandwich, two cookies, and a half-pint of milk. The food in this first section is contained, wrapped in wax paper, packed in a brown bag, and the meal is ingested alone. "Sucking the last / bit of milk at the bottom of the carton" suggests there is not enough here, there can be no second helping. As I wrote these lines I remembered how often in grade school I ate by myself, achingly lonely, surrounded and crowded by strangers, and hurried. But the poem's last section is one of healing, with friends feeding me like multiple loving mothers.

The poem did not come together easily. I had started an early group of notes for a poem titled "The Picnic Island" after the trip to Guadalajara to visit my mother's favorite cousin, my "Uncle Dick," (the subject of "Black Sheep, White Stars"). In 1989, when my mother and I traveled to Guadalajara to visit Dick, he had just finished what would be his last painting, which he called *The Picnic Island*. Occupying most of the canvas is an ark-shaped island, onto which pairs of giraffes, elephants, ponies, and camels are emerging from a boat. They saunter, two by two, on the sands, while high on a pavilion acrobats cavort. White bowls rest on bright yellow-green grass, and above a flowery, festooned banner, people sail up to the clouds in balloons. The colors are brilliant, pinks, yellows, greens, purples, and white, with accents of coral. Ocean and sky encircle the entire extravagant scene with blue; they, in turn, are ringed at the canvas's outer edge with a mossy fringe of black, suggesting the mouth of a cave, or tunnel, into which one is about to enter, taking a last look as one leaves the picnic island behind, or, from which one is about to emerge, bursting through from the darkness to all this pleasure. Dick had cataracts, and his sight was going. Surgery at that time in Mexico was expensive and risky. He said the painting was his idea of heaven, and that he would be there soon. He died the next year; our visit was just in time.

But his joy in living has remained with me. Arthritic, leaning hard on his cane, his sight clouded, he exuded *joie de vivre* in every word and gesture. Walking through the streets of Guadalajara, he viewed the most mundane human activities with wonder—I want to say "awe"—at the mystery of human life. For Dick, simply the sight of people moving through the streets, clustered in the plazas, was a picnic. All life was a picnic: the sounds of singing, laughing, and arguing, as people lingered on benches and at curbs, eating tamales and drinking Coronas, together, under the sun.

I can remember three picnics when I was growing up. Once while my father was out of town, my mother and sisters and I packed up snacks and drove to Mt. Lemmon above Tucson. Snapshots show us clowning, me at about fifteen, with a banana in my hand, about to take a bite. Of a much earlier picnic, with several other families, when I was about six, I have vaguely pleasant memories. But the one I remember most was the single picnic we took as a family. My father's tension made the entire event miserable. The pictures show my mother, who had prepared all the sandwiches, hard-boiled eggs, and thermoses, wearing an expression of forced jollity, but my sisters' and my faces look tentative, even fearful. Daddy was probably about to explode. Why, I do not know, but, in retrospect, I can not imagine his ever relaxing at a picnic table. What germs might we (and he) pick up? We had no way of knowing who had eaten there before us. He was responsible for us all, and who knows who might just drive up and—well, kidnap us, or shoot us? He sunburned easily, hated ants, insects, anything not squeaky clean.

So Uncle Dick's notion that picnics could be anywhere, anytime, took hold in me, loosened me. A picnic could be any pleasure taken as it comes.

It was the 1992 retreat with friends to South Padre Island that served as a catalyst for the poem. The long draft I include here shows how formless the poem was at first, how rambling. Still, the poem's sections were in place. As I worked at revisions, I tried for a structure that would unify the sections. I decided to use seven-line stanzas, which forced me to tighten and heighten the lines. I played with patterns I saw emerging: I could prepare the reader for the last section at the ocean by referring in the first stanza to the floor as a "sea of crowded children." The white of the ice cream (in reality, it was chocolate) echoes the white of the second section's Austin Healey. I tried to make the poem's effect as conversational and relaxed, as easy as the feeling of eating on the gently rocking train in France.

This is a carpe diem poem of sorts. "Seize the day," it says; here is a moment: take it, live it. Here is a morsel of pleasure: taste it, ingest it. Ultimately, I changed the poem's title from "The Picnic Island" to "Picnic Makings." We never know when they will come, how they will find us. Or where. On a beach, in a city, in a garden, on a kitchen table, in a hospital, or even a classroom. They are all around us, in the midst of our crowded lives, the ingredients of a picnic—these moments of intense life—the stuff of poems.

❖ WORKS CITED ❖

Allison, Alexander W., Herbert Harrows, Caesar R. Blake, Arthur J. Carr, Arthur M. Eastman, and Hubert M. English, Jr., eds. *The Norton Anthology of Poetry.* Revised Ed. New York: W. W. Norton, 1975.

Auden, W. H. *Selected Poetry of W. H. Auden.* 2nd Ed. New York: Vintage Books, 1971.

Brontë, Charlotte. *Jane Eyre.* New York: Random House, 1943.

Dickinson, Emily. *The Complete Poems of Emily Dickinson.* Ed. Thomas H. Johnson. Boston: Little, Brown, and Company, 1955.

Dickinson, Emily. *The Letters of Emily Dickinson.* Ed. Thomas H. Johnson. Cambridge: Harvard University Press, 1958.

Doty, Mark. *Still Life With Oysters and Lemon.* Boston: Beacon Press, 2001.

Ellman, Richard and Robert O'Clair, eds. *The Norton Anthology of Modern Poetry.* 2nd Ed. New York: W. W. Norton, 1988.

Fadiman, Anne. *Ex Libris: Confessions of a Common Reader.* New York: Farrar, Straus and Giroux, 1998.

Fenton, James. *The Strength of Poetry: Oxford Lectures.* New York: Farrar, Straus and Giroux, 2001.

Ferguson, Margaret, Mary Jo Salter, and Jon Stallworthy, eds. *The Norton Anthology of Poetry.* 4th Ed. New York: W. W. Norton, 1996.

Gilbert, Sandra M. *Acts of Attention: The Poems of D. H. Lawrence.* Ithaca and London: Cornell University Press, 1972.

Gilbert, Sandra M. and Susan Gubar. *The Madwoman in the Attic: The Woman Writer and the Nineteenth-Century Literary Imagination.* New Haven and London: Yale University Press, 1979.

Gregg, Linda. "The Art of Finding." *American Poet: The Journal of the Academy of American Poets* (Spring 2001): 34-35.

Hamblin, Richard. *The Invention of Clouds.* New York: Farrar, Straus, and Giroux, 2001.

Keats, John. *The Poems of Keats.* Ed. Miriam Allott. London: Longman

Group Limited, 1970.

Kunitz, Stanley. *Passing Through: The Later Poems, New and Selected*. New York: W. W. Norton, 1995.

Lawrence, D. H. *The Complete Poems of D. H. Lawrence*. Ed. Vivian de Sola Pinto and F. Warren Roberts. New York: Viking, 1971.

Shakespeare, William. *The Riverside Shakespeare*. Ed. G. Blakemore Evans. Boston: Houghton Mifflin, 1974.

Stevens, Wallace. *The Palm at the End of the Mind: Selected Poems and a Play*. Ed. Holly Stevens. New York: Vintage, 1990.

Thoreau, Henry D. *The Writings of Henry D. Thoreau*. Ed. J. Lyndon Shanley. Princeton: Princeton University Press, 1971.

Wharton, Edith. *Novels*. Ed. R. W. B. Lewis. New York: Literary Classics of the United States, 1985.

Whitman, Walt. *Leaves of Grass*. Ed. Sculley Bradley and Harold Blodgett. New York: W. W. Norton, 1973.

Williams, William Carlos. *Selected Poems*. Ed. Charles Tomlinson. New York: New Directions, 1985.

Yeats, William Butler. *Selected Poems and Three Plays*. Ed. M. L. Rosenthal. 3rd ed. New York: Macmillan, 1986.

❖ CREDITS ❖

"Baptism" is reprinted from *Let the Ice Speak* (Ithaca House Books, Greenfield Review Press, 1991). It was first published in *Concho River Review*, 4, No. 2 (1990).

"Black Sheep, Red Stars" is reprinted from *Let the Ice Speak*. It was first published in *Poetry*, 146, No. 1 (1985).

"Cumulonimbus Incus" and "Cumulus and Cirrus" were first published in *Poetry*, 178, No. 2 (2001). They were reprinted in *Poetry Daily*, www.poems.com, June 2, 2001.

"Exorcism of a Nightmare" was first published in *Poetry*, 138, No. 6 (1981).

"Father's Fish" is reprinted from *Let the Ice Speak*. It was first published in *Nimrod: International Journal of Contemporary Poetry and Fiction*, 34, No. 1 (1990).

"For Want of Dolls" is reprinted from *Let the Ice Speak*. It was first published in *The American Scholar*, 60, No. 3 (1991).

"From the Attic at Thornfield" is reprinted from *Let the Ice Speak*. It was first published in *Poetry*, 156, No. 2 (1990).

"My Father's Living Room" is reprinted from *Let the Ice Speak*. It was first published in *Chomo-Uri*, 5, No. 1 (1978).

"Needlepoint" is reprinted from *Winter Chickens* (Corona Publishing Company, 1990). It was first published in *Poet Lore*, 74, No. 1 (1979).

"Oatmeal and Morning Silence" was first published in *The Panhandler*, No. 22 (1990).

"Once More, Squam Lake" is reprinted from *Let the Ice Speak*. It was first published in *Passages North*, 8, No. 2 (1987).

"One Lemon" was first published in *Poet Lore*, 81, No. 3 (1986).

"Persephone's Version" is reprinted from *Let the Ice Speak*. It was first published in *Calyx*, 4, No. 3 (1980).

"Picnic Makings" is reprinted from *Way of Whiteness* (Wings Press, 2000).

"Practice" was first published in *California Quarterly*, No. 13/14 (1979).

"Schönbrunn Yellow" is reprinted from *Winter Chickens*. It was first published in *The American Scholar*, 54, No. 3 (1985). The essay was first published in the *San Antonio Current* (November 15, 2001).

"Swallow Watcher" is reprinted from *Winter Chickens*. It was first published in *The American Scholar*, 54, No. 3 (1985).

"To the Dogs, in Sofia" was first published in the *San Antonio Current* (June 28, 2001).

"Washing in Cremona at Ten O'Clock" is reprinted from *Winter Chickens*. It was first published in *PAX*, 2, No. 1 (1984).

"Way of Whiteness" is reprinted from *Way of Whiteness*. It was first published in *The Journal*, 19, No. 2 (1995).

"What Ceilings" was first published in *New Mexico Humanities Review*, No. 36 (1992).

❖ ABOUT THE AUTHOR ❖

WENDY BARKER is the author of three poetry collections and a chapbook. She has published a selection of translations from the poems of Rabindranath Tagore (with Saranindranath Tagore), as well as a scholarly study of Emily Dickinson and a collection of essays on the poet Ruth Stone (with Sandra M. Gilbert). She has received fellowships from the National Endowment for the Arts and the Rockefeller Foundation and a Fulbright lectureship, as well as The Mary Elinore Smith Poetry Prize from the editors of *The American Scholar*, the Literary Excellence Award from Gemini Ink, and the Violet Crown Book Award from the Writers' League of Texas (for her most recent collection of poetry, *Way of Whiteness*). She is a professor of English at the University of Texas at San Antonio.